Heal Your Aching Back

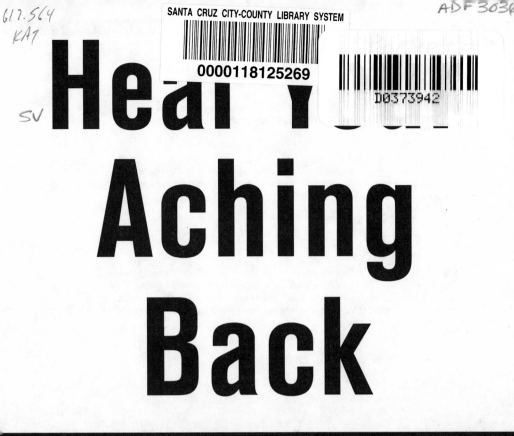

JEFFREY N. K TZ, M.D.
ASSOCIATE PROFESSOR, HAR   ICAL SCHOOL,
AND CODIRECTOR OF THE   E CENTER

AND **GLORI**

New York   Chicago   Lisbon   London   Madrid   Mexico City
Milan   New Delhi   Seoul   Singapore   Sydney   Toronto

Library of Congress Cataloging-in-Publication Data

Katz, Jeffrey Neil.
    Heal your aching back : what a Harvard doctor wants you to know about finding relief & keeping your back strong / by Jeffrey N. Katz, and Gloria Parkinson.
        p.   cm.
    Includes index.
    ISBN 0-07-146765-3
    1. Backache—Popular works.   2. Backache—Treatment—Popular works.
3. Backache—Prevention—Popular works.   4. Back—Care and hygiene—Popular works.   I. Parkinson, Gloria.   II. Title.

RD771.B217.K47   2007
617.5′64—dc22   2006036809

1 2 3 4 5 6 7 8 9 10 11 12 13 14 15 16 17 18 19 20 21 22 DOC/DOC 0 9 8 7

ISBN-13: 978-0-07-146765-0
ISBN-10:   0-07-146765-3

Interior design by Think Design Group, LLC
Figures on pages 38, 46, 47, 49, 65, 67, 211 copyright by Harriet Greenfield; pages 41, 44, 191, 193–195, 199, 200 (bottom), 234 by Barbara Cousins; pages 74, 134, 137 by Scott Leighton; pages 107, 163, 182, 189, 198 (top) by Jennifer Fairman; page 109 by Michael Linkinhoker; page 197 (top) by Doron Ben-Ami; pages 197 (bottom), 198 (bottom), 200 (top) by Matthew Holt; page 217 by Jesse Tarantino

The information contained in this book is intended to provide helpful and informative material on the subject addressed. It is not intended to serve as a replacement for professional medical advice. Any use of the information in this book is at the reader's discretion. The author, publisher, and the President and Fellows of Harvard College specifically disclaim any and all liability arising directly or indirectly from the use or application of any information contained in this book. A health-care professional should be consulted regarding your specific situation.

For Susy, Daniel, and Micah—
there is no stronger medicine than a home of love.
—Jeff

For Jim, my husband and best friend.
I cherish you, my love.
—Gloria

Contents

Preface   xi

Acknowledgments   xv

Part I   The Perplexities of Back Pain

Chapter 1

Bewildered by Your Back Pain?   3

    A Bewildering Condition   4

    Join the Crowd   8

    My Back's Killing Me   10

    You're in Charge   10

    Bewildered No More   16

Chapter 2

Factors Affecting Who Gets Back Pain   17

    Your Age   18

    Your Gender   19

    Pregnancy and Your Back   20

    Your Genes   21

    How You Work and Play   21

    Your Physical Makeup and Posture   22

    How You Deal Emotionally with Life's Slings and Arrows   23

    Other Risk Factors   24

Part II Understanding Back Pain

Chapter 3

The Workings of Your Back   29

The Wonder That Is Your Back   30
Your Back Through the Ages   36
Your Spine from Top to Bottom   37
Enough with the Anatomy!   50

Chapter 4

Why Your Back Hurts   53

Sprain-and-Strain Syndromes   58
Pinched (Compressed) Nerve Syndromes   63
Degenerative Disk Conditions   63
Degenerative Spinal Disease   70
Other Causes of Back Pain   71
Backache from Other Organs   77

Chapter 5

Getting a Diagnosis   79

How Should I Begin My Search?   80
Visit a Doctor, But Which One?   82
A Well-Prepared Medical History   83
The Value of the Physical Examination   85
When Imaging Tests Are Helpful   86
Other Diagnostic Procedures   95

Part III **Controlling Your Pain**

· ·

Chapter 6

Priority Number One: Relieving Your Pain   101

What Is Pain?   102
Pain: Out with the Old; In with the New   103
Classifying Your Pain by Its Duration   106
How Pain Works   107
Your Body's Natural Pain Relief Plan   111
Once More with Feeling: Describe Your Back Pain   113
Medicating Your Back Pain   116
Electrical Stimulation Therapies   136

Chapter 7

**Can Complementary Therapies
Help Your Aching Back?**   141

Get the Best: Is Your Therapist Qualified?   145
Spinal Manipulation   146
Massage   149
Acupuncture   152
Mind-Body Therapies   154
Complementary Exercise Programs   164
Other Complementary Pain Treatments   167
Glucosamine and Chondroitin Sulfate Supplements   168
Herbal Products and Back Pain   169
A Prudent Approach   172

Part IV Managing Your Back Condition

Chapter 8

Nonsurgical Treatments for Your Backache   175

Your Back's Capacity to Heal Itself   176

Waiting Out Acute Back Pain   177

Getting Going Again   182

Sign Up with an Exercise Professional   184

Principles of Rehabilitative Exercise for Back Pain   186

Strengthening and Stretching the Muscles of Your Back   190

Low-Impact Aerobic Exercises for Acute Back Pain   201

Chapter 9

Is Surgery Right for You?   203

How Do You Decide?   203

Do You Meet Surgical Criteria?   206

Weighing Surgical Risks and Benefits   206

Surgery for Disk Disease   208

Surgery for Compression (Osteoporotic) Fractures   214

Surgery for Lumbar Spinal Stenosis   217

Spinal Fusion Surgery   218

Surgery for Other Back Problems   220

Knowing When You're Ready to Decide   222

Chapter 10

Preventing a Repeat Episode   225

Stay Fit   225
Getting in the Exercise Groove   227
Watch Your Weight   229
Kick the Smoking Habit   231
The Everyday Business of Moving and Sitting   231

Chapter 11

When Pain Persists   239

Pain That Takes on a Life of Its Own   239
What Is Debilitating Chronic Pain?   240
Who's at Risk?   241
What Can Be Done for Patients with Chronic Pain?   243

Glossary   247

Additional Resources   255

Index   261

Preface

Although Gloria Parkinson and I wrote this book together in 2005–6, the story began for me in the spring of 1984, when I was completing my final year of medical school. One March evening I fell hard in an intramural basketball game and developed pain and muscle spasm in my lower back. I had no numbness, tingling, or pain with coughing or sneezing, and the pain did not travel to my legs. But for weeks I was unable to do much except hobble around very slowly because of the pain I felt.

By the time you finish Chapter 4, you'll recognize that I had garden-variety back sprain. And by the end of Chapter 8, you'll know that this problem generally takes care of itself over a period of weeks and can be diagnosed and managed correctly without x-rays or other imaging tests. Further, you'll appreciate that the most effective approach to garden-variety back pain is simply to remain as active as possible within the boundaries of your pain; to maintain your social roles at home, work, or school as best you can; to use simple measures such as heat, cold, acetaminophen, and ibuprofen; and, most important, to let go of your fear. The problem will get better.

I wish I had known these things back in 1984. At the time of my injury, I had completed all but two months of medical school at one of the most prestigious medical institutions in the world. Yet amazingly, I had never met a patient with back pain, nor had I read or heard anything about it in the formal curriculum. I had a vague sense that back pain was a chronic problem that would forever prevent me from doing athletics and limit me at work. As you can imagine, I was quite distressed. I sought care and was directed to a highly regarded rheumatologist (a specialist in arthritis and other musculoskeletal problems) who told me that I should lie flat on my back as often as possible for as long as possible, until the situation got better. I was sent for radiographs of the spine, which were normal. I was referred to an orthopedic surgeon who concluded surgery was not necessary.

I recall vividly spending the Passover Seders (festive dinners) in April 1984 lying on the carpeted floor in my in-laws' home, staring at the shoes of various guests sitting around the dining room table. I tentatively got up for key prayers and to have a bite to eat, but spent most of the evening, as so many others that spring, lying flat on the floor. I felt fearful, especially with a medical internship just a few weeks away. Would I be able to do it? And I felt embarrassed by my disability.

Although my pain persisted, graduation came and I had to choose between continuing the prescribed activity limitation and bed rest or getting on with my work as a medical intern. I'm a pragmatic person and, frankly, had begun to doubt the effectiveness of rest and immobility. So I set off to work as a medical intern in a busy city hospital. I spent that summer on my feet day and night. By August my back pain was virtually gone.

It comes back every now and then. Like most people with back pain, I have recurrent episodes. Mine typically occur two or three times a year. But I know what to do with these bouts of pain: I continue to walk, work, stretch, and stay busy. And in between bouts I exercise regularly, usually four times each week.

Viewed by today's standards, virtually everything the medical professionals did for me and my back pain in 1984 was wrong, or unnecessary, or both. There was no need for early x-rays or referral to a specialist and a surgeon. The specialist prescribed disability, failed to educate, and failed to reassure. I knew my chosen profession was capable of better.

Over the next decade, I chose to become a rheumatologist. Influenced by my personal experience and awakened awareness of the gaping hole in medical care, I focused my research and clinical interests on regional musculoskeletal pain problems, particularly back pain. I did a rheumatology fellowship at Brigham and Women's Hospital, a teaching hospital affiliated with Harvard Medical School, in Boston. In 1992, shortly after completing my fellowship, I was invited to codirect the Brigham Spine Center, a referral unit for patients with lumbar, thoracic, and cervical spine problems. I've been meeting with patients in the Spine Center every Friday morning for fifteen years. I've heard countless stories from patients with all sorts of back-pain problems. Along the way I have done research on low-back pain, read the growing literature on low-back and neck pain voraciously, and attended many conferences dedicated to back pain. I try to teach what I have learned to many students, residents, and postdoctoral fellows at Brigham and Women's Hospital and Harvard Medical School.

The most important audience, however, is you, the reader. You've picked up this book because you likely have back pain, have had it previously, or have friends or family members who have back pain. My hope is that in reading this book you will become more knowledgeable and less fearful about back pain and its natural history and treatments.

In the upcoming chapters we'll present you with the best information we can find about the epidemiology, natural history, and treatment of back-pain syndromes. These include garden-variety back pain as well as herniated-disk syndromes, spinal stenosis, spondylolisthesis, and other conditions affecting the lumbar and cervical spine. There isn't a quick fix for back pain. First you have to understand the nuances of your back condition. Only then can you consider your management options. With this in mind, Gloria and I have organized this book in four parts. Part I looks at the big picture of back pain, including who is more likely to be a back-pain sufferer. Part II provides you with an understanding of your back: why it might hurt and the challenges of getting a specific diagnosis.

Part III describes the cornerstone of back-pain management—traditional and nontraditional approaches to pain control. After all, until you get pain relief, you can't begin to consider your other treatment options. Only after this exhaustive foundation work do we embark on Part IV, which discusses the management of your back condition, including the all-important role of exercise in rehabilitation and the prevention of recurrences; and when to consider surgery for your back problem. In other words, the advice in this book builds logically on your understanding of the complexities of your situation. Put another way: first understand; then act.

When I first became a back-pain patient in 1984, there was little research on back pain. The seminal article showing that two days of bed rest was preferable to seven had not yet been published. In the last two decades there have been thousands of articles on back pain. Our goal is to present you this body of evidence, sprinkled with lessons I've learned in my own practice, particularly in areas where the literature is thinnest. Above all, my aim is for you to feel confident that you will be able to cope calmly and intelligently with an episode of back pain should you have one.

Acknowledgments

As you read in the Preface, I owe my interest in low-back pain, ironically, to some very fine physicians who treated me for this problem more than twenty years ago and did mostly everything "wrong." Of course they did the best they could; and their treatment was state of the art at the time. But it seemed apparent to me then, and is completely clear to me now, that the medical profession's understanding and management of low-back pain was primitive at the time I was completing my medical training.

As it came time for me to choose my specialty and specific areas of interest, I found myself fascinated with the simple musculoskeletal problems that we all have to confront many times in our lives. I'm talking about back pain, neck pain, and other regional pain problems involving the shoulders, hands and wrists, hips, knees, ankles, and feet. Some of these syndromes have specific terms such as bursitis and tendonitis; others have a confusing array of names. The common denominator is that these problems are painful, disabling, costly, highly prevalent—and woefully understudied. These musculoskeletal problems have been my passion since I started seeing patients as a rheumatologist in 1987 at Brigham and Women's Hospital. Musculoskeletal problems have also been the focus of my clinical research.

I cannot possibly thank all the people who helped position me to write this book, or who helped in its writing and production. But several individuals stand out. The first is Dr. Stephen J. Lipson, an exceptional orthopedic spine surgeon and an exceptional human being whom I met in 1987 when I arrived at Brigham and Women's. Steve is about the best doctor I have ever known. His intimate, encyclopedic knowledge of spinal disorders and the human condition, and his generosity with patients and colleagues remain ideals to which I aspire daily. Steve's passionate interest in chronic low-back pain in the middle-aged and elderly ignited my own lifelong engagement in these areas. His courageous struggle to carry on with his work despite his own chronic illness has been a special inspiration to me.

Gloria and I have tried to share with the reader the best evidence available in the diagnosis and management of low-back pain. I cannot possibly acknowledge all of the many dedicated scholars who helped to develop the modern basis of spine care. But I would like to thank three individuals—Drs. John Frymoyer, Richard Deyo, and James Weinstein—each giants in the field, who reached out to me to help me launch my own research and clinical career. As they would modestly point out, their contributions were made possible by their own mentors and may become obsolete by the insights of their students. Fair enough. Still, it's hard for me to imagine three more dedicated, insightful mentors and scholars than John, Rick, and Jim, and I celebrate them here.

The Brigham and Women's Hospital is a rich environment in which to mature as a scholar and clinician. Over the course of two decades, my own development as a "back-pain expert" has been nurtured by countless conversations with clinical colleagues dedicated to spine care including Drs. Simon Helfgott, Zacharia Isaac, John Carrino, Greg Brick, and many others. Back in 1992, my department chair, Dr. K. Frank Austen, invited me to codirect the Brigham Spine Center. This has been a wonderfully rich opportunity for which I am extremely grateful. I also thank Drs. Matthew Liang, Michael Brenner, and Thomas Thornhill, who supported my vision of developing research and clinical expertise in back pain and other regional musculoskeletal disorders.

Medicine is described aridly in texts but lived richly in the clinic, one patient at a time. Over the last nineteen years I have had the privilege of working with thousands of patients who suffer from low-back pain. Some I saw just once for a self-limited problem; others I have seen for more than a decade. Each patient has taught me something different and special, and I thank them all. And since patients are the best teachers, at various times throughout the book Gloria and I use patient vignettes to illustrate points. These vignettes are composites, based on patients I have seen in my practice over the years. Although the names have been changed, the problems and solutions described are real.

This book was the inspiration of Dr. Anthony Komaroff, Director of Harvard Health Publications. In 2005 Tony asked me if I thought there was anything new to say about low-back pain and whether I'd like to be the one to say it. This was a wonderful offer and I hope the book lives up to Tony's own high standards of scholarly and clinical excellence. The other wonderful gift from Tony was his pairing me with Gloria Parkinson. As the reader of this book will soon appreciate, Gloria is an exceptionally talented writer. Permit me to tell you that she is also dedicated, kind, witty, and wonderfully good company. Gloria and I enjoyed writing this book together and hope that the reader has fun reading it.

Finally, Gloria and I thank the editorial staff of Harvard Health Publications, especially Raquel Schott for her immense patience as Gloria and I worked through our iterative process in the creation of this book.

Part I

The Perplexities of Back Pain

Chapter 1

Bewildered by
Your Back Pain?

You've most likely opened this book because your back hurts. Maybe you've had back pain for a matter of weeks; maybe you're a longtime sufferer; or maybe you're wondering about surgery. Another possibility is that you previously had a bout of back pain and made a full recovery. Then suddenly, for no apparent reason, you wake in the morning, prepared to spring into your day, and you're in agony. If you recognize yourself in any of these scenarios, this book is for you.

Whether you're having recurring bouts of back pain or you're one of those unfortunate people who have endured persistent back pain for more than six months, chances are you've already made the rounds of doctors and may even have heard several different opinions about how to treat your back problem. In addition, well-meaning family members and friends may have proffered all sorts of helpful suggestions. Unfortunately, these suggestions may have been confusingly contradictory. One person may have told you to stay in bed, while another advised against staying in bed. Someone may have told you to exercise your way back to a pain-free life, the "no pain, no gain" approach to your situation. Somebody else, on the other hand, might have recommended doing absolutely nothing physical until you feel better and thereafter doing next to nothing—to guard against a relapse. You may also have heard a wide range of advice about surgery, with advocates advising surgery as soon as possible and naysayers warning you that surgery should be your last resort when everything else has failed. Not surprisingly, you come away from these conversations with not only a painful back but also a spinning head! If you've been on the receiving end of such confusing advice, this book is for you.

A Bewildering Condition

If you're feeling bewildered about how to manage your back pain, you're in good company. Many of my patients are similarly confused when they are referred to me, as are the doctors who referred them. Let me share with you a fairly common patient story that illustrates just how frustrating getting a diagnosis and a recommended treatment plan can be. Theresa is a woman in her forties who developed back pain without provocation. With three very active young children to take care of, back pain was not good news. By the time she walked into my office, Theresa was feeling decidedly frazzled. One doctor had told her she had a disk problem; another told her that her disks were fine and the problem was the ligaments in her back. Yet another doctor said there didn't seem to be anything wrong with her back at all—despite the fact that Theresa was in pain. To make matters worse, she'd received a range of different treatment recommendations, from steroid injections to medications to exercises. Needless to say, she was confused and frustrated, with no idea whom she should listen to or what advice she should follow. We'll be returning to Theresa later in the book, but for now know that ultimately Theresa was helped to make decisions that were right for her and that she is now engaged in many of the family and community activities she enjoys.

If Theresa's experience of going from doctor to doctor and coming away no wiser matches yours, you might think back-pain doctors are not up to snuff. But that's not true. It's important to appreciate that your doctor may well be feeling as frustrated as you. A major stumbling block for doctors and patients alike is that in the United States there have been no recent national guidelines for the diagnosis and treatment of back pain. Although the Agency for Health Care Policy and Research published low-back-pain guidelines in 1992, these have not been updated. And fourteen years is a long time in the history of a medical condition. There has been a lot of new research in that period. Another consideration relates to doctors who specialize in back pain. While specialists can be invaluable, seeing a medical specialist at the start of your back-pain episode is sometimes not as helpful as you might wish. This sounds contrary, but it's a matter of focus. A specialist tends to look for anomalies that explain the problem in terms of his or her specialty. So a doctor who specializes in orthopedics may see an orthopedic abnormality, for example, a slight problem in alignment of the vertebrae, and be convinced the problem is orthopedic in nature. Similarly, a neurologist who specializes in problems of the nervous system may see a nerve problem. This explains some of the diagnostic discrepancies and mixed-message treatment recommendations back-pain sufferers receive.

But whatever the reason, doctors vary markedly in the tests they order and the treatments they recommend for back pain. This has led to diagnostic and treatment inconsistencies and contradictions. Little wonder then that patients, especially those like Theresa who have made the rounds, become bewildered and discouraged.

The good news, however, is that back-pain times "are a changin.'" During the past decade or so, researchers have shed invaluable light on the discomforts and diseases of the spine. They've evaluated the pluses and minuses of improved diagnostic approaches for back pain, especially the limitations of computed tomography (CT) and magnetic resonance imaging (MRI) scans. They've monitored the several new or fine-tuned back-treatment options that have become available. The best evidence available today suggests that patients with back pain should remain as active as possible. So back-pain treatments these days attempt to get you going again as soon as is reasonable for the degree of pain you are experiencing. All in all, application of this research has helped most back-pain sufferers get up and about and return to their normal lives more quickly than previously. But like much good news, it's taken a while to spread, which explains the contradictory advice back-pain sufferers sometimes receive.

Getting the Word Out

Medicine moves forward when doctors and patients know what's going on. In this "information age" there's lots of information a fingertip away on your computer. But how do you and your doctor know what's reliable and up-to-date and what isn't? One way of keeping up with the latest research is by reading the rigorously conducted, randomized scientific studies designed to show what works and, very importantly, what doesn't seem to work. Well-designed studies help doctors stay in touch with the latest research findings and ticklish research questions that remain unanswered. Studies are typically disseminated via written scientific papers published in print or electronic format in reputable professional scientific journals. Although the main readership for studies is other doctors working in the field, anyone so inclined can read them. The only drawback for lay people is that you need access to a well-stocked medical library or to be prepared to pay a download fee if you go to the journal publisher online.

Once the word is out in a study, though, it's not the final word. Studies build on studies, with other researchers testing the findings of one study, amending the conclusions of another, or sleuthing out some detail in yet another, which then leads to a further line of investigation. It's a never-ending process.

All this activity would be difficult to keep up with were it not for periodic reviews of past studies. Every so often a group of researchers will publish a review that looks back over several years of studies. This has the effect of pulling the research together in a way that redraws or repaints the lines of the ballpark.

Two very important reviews on low-back pain published by the *New England Journal of Medicine* in 2001 and 2005, respectively, are "Low Back Pain" by Richard A. Deyo of the Department of Medicine at the University of Washington and James N. Weinstein of the Department of Orthopedic Surgery at Dartmouth Medical School, and "Persistent Low Back Pain" by Eugene J. Carragee of the Department of Orthopedic Surgery at Stanford University. These two recent reviews looked at low-back-pain research over the past fifteen or so years and pulled into sharp resolution the consensus findings that are the basis of today's diagnostic and treatment approaches. These findings are what I follow in my back-pain practice and they are the basis of much of my advice in this book.

As well as receiving conflicting advice, the other major bewildering aspect of dealing with back pain is that most of us will never know the specific reason why our backs hurt. Amazing though this sounds, especially in modern medicine's high-tech diagnostic environment, it's usually impossible to pinpoint the precise cause of a back problem. In Chapter 5, I'll explain why this is so. Fortunately this inability to be diagnostically definitive doesn't mean your back pain can't be treated. It can, and very successfully. This might seem like just another contradiction, but unlike the contradictions that end in confusion, today there is a very clear path leading to a back-pain treatment that will work for you. The key is to know the *location* and *type* of back pain you have. With these coordinates you and your doctor can map out a treatment plan that suits your particular back problem and, importantly, your personality and lifestyle requirements.

My goal in this book is to help you recognize the where and what of your back pain and introduce you to the various treatment options that will restore your get-up-and-go.

Join the Crowd

First, take comfort in knowing you're not alone. An enormous number of people have back problems of one type or another. Let's consider neck and back pain separately and appreciate the pervasiveness of each in society. Doctors estimate that seven out of ten people in the United States will be troubled by some type of *neck pain* at some point in their lives. One in ten adults has neck pain right now, and for one in twenty the pain is sufficiently intense to limit that person's ability to work and play.

An even larger number of us have a *low-back-pain* problem. About 80 percent of the U.S. population will suffer from low-back pain at some point. The condition is the fifth most common reason why people visit their doctors. As well as the pain and inconvenience, low-back pain disrupts lives in other ways. For example, it hits individual paychecks and takes a sizable bite out

Table 1.1

Number of Americans with Chronic Diseases

Disease	Number in Millions
Low-back pain	**63.2**
Hypertension	41.8
Arthritis	41.2
Sinusitis	35.5
Neck pain	**34.0**
Migraines/severe headaches	33.9
Heart disease	23.5
Asthma	22.2
Hay fever	20.4
Stomach ulcers	18.9
Diabetes	13.0

SOURCE: CDC. Summary Health Statistics for U.S. Adults: National Interview Survey, 2001.

of government spending. At any given time, one in four American workers will be having a bout of low-back pain. Not surprisingly, low-back pain is one of the main reasons people miss work. It's also the most common cause of work-related disability in Americans under forty-five years of age. When everything is added up, low-back pain costs a staggering 26-plus billion dollars a year. Another way of showing how pervasive back pain is in our society is to compare back pain with other chronic diseases (see Table 1.1). Looked at this way, in the United States low-back pain is a clear front-runner, with neck pain coming in at number five. In other countries where such records are kept, back pain is also a major health problem.

My Back's Killing Me

You may have uttered these words when your back was acting up, but they're unlikely to be true. Although it can certainly be extremely painful, as long as back pain isn't a secondary symptom of an underlying serious condition, such as cancer or infection, it isn't a potentially terminal condition.

Back pain does not describe a single entity. Rather *back pain* is an umbrella term that includes a number of discrete medical conditions, which can range in severity. At one end of the range, a bout of back pain is a transient, albeit painful, condition that will get better on its own without the need for professional medical help. At the other end of the range, back pain is an indication of a serious condition needing immediate medical attention. Between these two extremes are a number of longer-lasting back conditions that to varying degrees restrict your activities, diminish the quality of your life, and make you thoroughly miserable. As well as living with long-lasting back pain, some people experience other debilitating repercussions, such as depression. These more long-lasting back problems require carefully thought-through treatment approaches. In some instances, more than one treatment option is available, which means you should familiarize yourself with the pros and cons of all the options.

You're in Charge

A very important aspect of managing your back pain is understanding that it's *your* back pain. You're in charge. This shift to patient-centered management is happening in many areas of medicine. But taking control of their treatment management is particularly appropriate for people with back pain. As individuals we feel pain differently. A tolerable degree of pain for one person may be intolerable for someone else. Our lifestyles are different in terms of physical demands and life/work responsibilities. Some of us have more time than others to "wait out" a back problem. Others have to be back in the swing of things as soon as possible. These and similar considerations affect treatment decisions.

Being in charge means you need to know what you're in charge of. The successful resolution of a back-pain problem depends to some extent on understanding a number of back-pain concepts. We'll be looking at these concepts in detail in later chapters, but to give you a sense of the whole landscape before we embark on our journey, here's a road map.

Location! Location! Location!

Location is an important diagnostic and treatment consideration. Although back problems can develop anywhere in your back, there are times when treatment varies depending on where the problem is. Because location matters, your doctor will categorize your back pain as either neck pain or low-back pain. You will sometimes hear neck pain referred to as *cervical pain* because of its location in the upper part of the spine called the *cervical spine*. Similarly, low-back pain is sometimes referred to as *lumbar pain* because the pain is located in the lower, or lumbar, region of the spine. If you have neck (cervical) pain, your doctor will ask whether it radiates to your arms. Similarly, if you have low-back (lumbar) pain, your doctor will ask if it radiates to your buttocks, thighs, lower legs, and feet. Why so nosy? Location! Turns out that the location of the pain provides an invaluable clue about the cause of the discomfort, the likely course it will take, and the best types of treatment.

Know Your Type of Back Problem

Both neck pain and low-back pain can be attributed to a number of different types of problems or syndromes. The type of back problem you have determines your treatment. Like well-matched dance partners, when the treatment is appropriate for the type of problem, recovery should go smoothly. With a mismatch, recovery may falter and stumble. Here's an overview of the types of back problems I'll talk about in detail in later chapters.

- **Sprain-and-strain syndrome** refers to back pain that results from spraining or straining the soft tissues of the back, principally, but not only, muscles and ligaments. Sprains and strains are by far the most common cause of back pain. Although quite painful, they usually clear up on their own in a matter of weeks without requiring professional medical attention. The downside of this type of back pain is that it frequently recurs—often without warning. This means that if you have low-back pain or sprain, preventing subsequent episodes should be the primary goal of your recovery plan. In this sprain-and-strain-syndrome category we also include back pain that seems to result from arthritis of the small joints of the back. It's difficult to distinguish between the soft-tissue pain of muscles and ligaments and spinal-joint pain. Since they probably exist together in some patients and since they both present with pain in the middle of your lower back, we will discuss them together.

- **Pinched (compression) nerve syndromes** are the next most common cause of back problems. These syndromes include anything that compresses nerves. Examples include disk problems such as when a herniated disk causes radiating pain because it's compressing a sciatic nerve (sciatica). Another example is spinal stenosis, which occurs when a narrowing of the spinal column puts pressure on the nerves it houses. Although both these painful conditions are due to nerve compression, they're treated differently.

- **Red flag (emergency) situations** belong in a category all their own because they require immediate medical attention. Red flag situations include back pain due to infection, tumor, fracture, and a severe nerve compression condition involving the nerves of the bladder and rectum known as *cauda equina syndrome.* In cases of infection, tumor, and fracture, swift measures should be taken to treat these underlying causes of the back pain. Similarly prompt action is necessary in the case of cauda equina syndrome to avoid permanent nerve damage. Although you should be aware of the possibility of red flag situations, fortunately they are relatively uncommon compared to sprain-and-strain and pinched nerve syndromes.

- **Congenital back diseases or back conditions acquired early in life** do happen, but again they are far less common than sprain-and-strain and pinched nerve syndromes. Childhood scoliosis, a curvature of the spine, comes under this banner.

- **Metabolic back disease** can happen when the bone of the vertebrae that makes up the spinal column changes. The most common metabolic back disease is osteoporosis, a condition that causes thinning of bones and frequently fractures, especially in older women. Other metabolic bone diseases, such as Paget's disease, are rare causes of back pain.

- **Miscellaneous** is a catchall category of relatively unusual back disorders. Spondylitis, for example, is an inflammatory back disease that we include in this miscellaneous category.

As you can appreciate, there's quite an array of back problems. And this list is not complete. But since sprain-and-strain and pinched nerve syndromes are far and away what most people suffer from, much of this book will be devoted to the diagnosis, treatment, and prevention of back problems associated with these two categories.

Nature Will Take Her Course

Regardless of the type of back problem you have and where it is located, the third piece of information you need to know before embarking on a specific treatment approach is the natural history of your back problem. In other words, how long would you be likely to have the problem if it were left untreated? This is not a pie-in-the-sky notion. We now have scientific information that can predict the natural histories of the various types of back pain. This is very useful, practical information that back-pain sufferers should include in their deliberations about which treatment approach would be best for them. Natural history information is especially helpful if you're considering a surgical option. If the natural history of your back problem predicts a relatively short duration of symptoms, you might decide to hold off on surgery and adopt a wait-and-watch approach. An anticipated longer duration might tip the balance in favor of surgery.

Acute Versus Chronic Pain

"Acute" and "chronic" relate to the length of time you experience pain. Acute back pain is painful at the onset, but the pain is relatively short-lived. For most people, their symptoms improve within days or a couple of weeks, leading to a complete recovery within three to seven months. Chronic pain, however, means that the pain has lasted six months or more. Here, the prognosis is not as good. Patients who have had pain for six months are unlikely to get better quickly. Knowing the nature of your pain is another important part of how you decide which treatment approach to adopt.

Many Factors Are Associated with Back Pain; Many Approaches Are Used to Treat It

Back-pain doctors hesitate to discuss "causes" of back pain, because frankly it's often difficult to say why an episode of pain occurred. But we know from studies of many patients with back pain that some factors are commonly associated with the problem. For example, your back pain may have resulted from something physical, such as an injury or a fall. It may be the result of your lifestyle. You may be sedentary at work and play and over time your body has become deconditioned. Perhaps there are work-associated difficulties. Low pay and job dissatisfaction have been shown to influ-

The First Scientific Paper on Back Pain

The study of back pain has had a long and distinguished history, but you might be surprised to know quite how long. The first orthopedic paper we know of was written more than 4,630 years ago—on papyrus. The Egyptian Imhotep (2686–2613 B.C.) was a multitalented man who served the second pharaoh of the Third Dynasty. As well as being an astronomer, magician, priest, and architect, Imhotep was an extremely sharp-eyed physician who meticulously recorded his observations. The papyrus, found in a pharaoh's tomb in Thebes, describes bone lesions, including those of the spine. In addition to noting sprains and dislocations, Imhotep made the connection between a severed spinal cord and paralysis, although he didn't know the reason why. That knowledge came much later.

ence back problems. And then there's your genes. You may have a family predisposition to develop certain back problems. Some of these things you can do something about; others you can't.

Since many factors can influence the onset of back pain, treatment also comes in several shapes and sizes. Often the best outcome is achieved with a combination of treatments, rather than with a single treatment approach. Healing your back takes effort. Making sure your back stays healthy takes more effort.

Bewildered No More

Back pain has bothered humans for a very long time. During the course of its history, some treatment suggestions have admittedly not been ideal. But today there are many effective treatment strategies available that can relieve your discomfort, enable you to resume your activities, and help prevent a recurrence of your problem. In consultation with your doctor you can make informed decisions that will lead to good outcomes. In the upcoming chapters we'll be looking at the scientifically supported knowledge and practices that will influence your decisions.

Chapter 2

Factors Affecting Who Gets Back Pain

A question many of my patients ask when they have back pain is, "Why me?" I reassure them they're not alone. Unfortunately, most of us are likely to have at least one episode of back pain at some point in our lives (see Figure 2.1). After the common cold, lumbar back pain, for instance, is the second most frequent cause of Americans taking time off work. Other Western industrialized countries have documented similarly large numbers of lost workdays due to back problems. Although for most of us our backache is a finite problem, while it lasts it can be quite painful and very inconvenient in terms of work and leisure time.

Given the pervasiveness of back problems, can your doctor tell you if you are more likely to be at risk? Although we can't predict with certainty, research has found that some activities, health problems, demographic factors, and other characteristics put you at greater risk for developing back problems. Of course, some people with back pain don't have these risk factors, yet they still develop

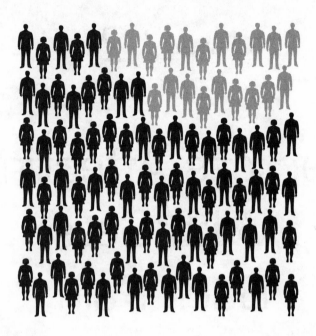

Figure 2.1

In Good Company

About 80 percent of adult Americans will experience at least one episode of low-back pain during their lives.

backache. The evidence then is not perfect, but it does provide very useful pointers about risk factors so you can consider how they might apply to you and help you lower the chance that you'll have back problems.

Your Age

Age gets blamed for many things, but it may surprise you to know that people are most likely to suffer from low-back pain between ages twenty and forty. Although no one knows for certain, most back doctors think a couple of factors influence why these are the peak years for back problems. First, these tend to be very active decades for people, and this tendency increases the opportunity for back injuries. Second, degenerative changes in disks and other spinal structures are already under way by the time we reach our third and fourth decades of life. Although these changes don't necessarily cause pain, and you can't conclude that changes due to wear and tear are the source of your pain, as we'll see in Chapter 5, they can make your back more vulnerable to injury. In other words, twenty to forty are the years we begin to pay for how we've treated our backs in terms of lifestyle, sports activities, bad lifting habits, and so on. While back problems may be more common in people in their middle years, in older individuals back-pain attacks are more severe and longer lasting, and perhaps for this reason more memorable.

Your Gender

Studies suggest that men and women are equally plagued by back pain. However, in Western industrialized societies, men are more apt to have disk problems; and men are more likely to be treated surgically. Men probably have more disk problems because more men than women are working in jobs that involve heavy lifting, pushing, and pulling. Men may have more surgery because they have more severe low-back pain. There are probably other reasons for the discrepancy in surgery rates between the genders. Men may simply be more willing to have surgery because they can get back to normal sooner, whether that means returning to work or to the golf course. Research has also shown that women tend to be more cautious around many types of surgeries—spinal or other—preferring to give less-invasive treatment options a chance before turning to surgery. Women may feel they can't afford the time to be immobile while they recuperate from surgery because of their caretaking responsibilities. It's also possible that doctors are unconsciously biased toward recommending surgery to men more often than to women.

Sometimes it's impossible to know if there truly are gender differences regarding certain conditions. Some studies, for instance, suggest that men are three times more likely to develop ankylosing spondylitis, a severe but uncommon form of inflammatory arthritis that affects the spine. Other studies, however, found that men and women are equally afflicted. Women, though, are often less severely affected, and so not diagnosed as often.

On the other hand, osteoporosis (loss of bone density and strength) clearly affects women more often than men, especially older women. The reason is that postmenopausal women lose the protection of estrogen and undergo a period of rapid bone loss, which can cause severe weakening of vertebrae and may eventually lead to painful vertebral compression fractures. Men, on the whole, don't experience such rapid bone loss. Older women are also more susceptible than men to degenerative arthritis (osteoarthritis), including degenerative arthritis of the spine, a condition that involves the vertebral joints. Degenerative spondylolisthesis, an abnormal forward displacement of a vertebra relative to the one below it caused by erosion of the facet joints, also affects women more than men.

Pregnancy and Your Back

Pregnancy often causes backache in the lumbar spine region, especially in the final trimester. Although for most women the discomfort disappears after childbirth, it may become a chronic condition for an unfortunate few. The exact reason that low-back pain occurs after childbirth is not known. It could be a combination of factors: ligaments loosen during the third trimester; abdominal muscles stretch and weaken; and carrying the fetus and giving birth stress the back. And as any mom can vouch, caring for and carrying an infant or small child further tax the back.

Your Genes

Genes may influence who develops back problems possibly more than any other factor. Intervertebral disk defects, for example, are more common in some families. A hereditary difference in the chemical makeup of disks may render them more prone to degenerative change or herniation, which can trigger back pain. Ankylosing spondylitis and spondylolisthesis—the inflammatory disease of the spine and the abnormal forward displacement of a vertebra I mentioned earlier—likewise seem to run in families.

How You Work and Play

Certain jobs and activities put a greater strain on your back. Driving motor vehicles is notoriously hard on your back, for instance, because it involves prolonged periods of sitting and exposure to vibration. The stationary positions necessary for office work—from typing to computer programming to telephone stock-trading—can also eventually take a toll on your back regardless of your age.

Several other job-related activities increase the likelihood of future back problems. These activities include:

- Lifting or forceful movements such as pulling and pushing
- Frequent bending or twisting of the back
- Heavy physical exertion

- Maintaining the same position for long periods
- Repetitive motion patterns
- Exposure to incessant vibration

Your Physical Makeup and Posture

Your build, weight, and height seem to have little to do with your likelihood of developing back pain, although being overweight puts you at increased risk of having your symptoms return. Even a moderate difference in leg length (up to three-quarters of an inch), which you might think would lead to stress on at least the lower part of your spine, has no proven adverse effect on the lower back.

Historically, the finger has been pointed at poor posture as a cause of backache. But in spite of your mother's admonition to "sit up straight," experts now agree that in most cases posture alone—whether bad or good—will neither predispose you to back pain nor shield you from it. Slumping and slouching don't seem to have much effect on the basic health of your spine. Even moderate scoliosis (a lateral, or sideways, congenital curvature of the spine) usually doesn't produce chronic back discomfort. But before you drop your shoulders and droop into your chair, it's important to note that poor posture can exacerbate existing back pain. Improving your body mechanics can help relieve your symptoms and prevent recurrences.

On the other hand, lack of head and neck alignment when sitting at the computer or conversing with the telephone wedged between your ear and your shoulder can put undue strain on the swath of trapezius muscles in your upper back, which can become painful and may also give you a headache.

How You Deal Emotionally with Life's Slings and Arrows

A growing body of evidence shows that our emotions and psychological well-being have a significant influence on our physical health. You'll probably not be surprised to learn that psychological factors can affect our experience of back pain; and, in turn, back pain can lead to worry, anxiety, and depression. Although study population and methods vary, in general the research has shown that psychological factors such as stress, anxiety, and negative mood and emotions (such as "catastrophizing" an event rather than taking it in your stride) all increase the likelihood of developing acute or chronic back pain.

Such psychological factors seem to be especially important in determining whether an acute bout of back pain will become a longer-lasting chronic problem. One review of studies that examined psychological factors and back pain found that people who were distressed or depressed were more likely to develop chronic back pain than others. The reasons why this should be so are not completely understood, but the current scientific speculation is that two mechanisms may be involved.

The first is behavioral. A person suffering from acute pain in the lower back, for example, may start to become overly careful and limit movement to avoid triggering additional pain. Yet the unnatural stiffness and inactivity that such guarded movements promote ultimately worsen the situation. This problem, known as "fear avoidance," is especially common in patients who are anxious and depressed. The second possibility relates to biochemistry. The symptoms of chronic pain and depression share some of the same biochemical roots. The neurotransmitters serotonin and norepinephrine, for example, are involved not only in mood disorders, such as depression, but are also important in producing the sensation of pain.

Whatever the reasons, fortunately, this psychological spiral, whereby back pain begets psychological distress, which further exacerbates back pain, can be reversed. By changing the behaviors and addressing the emotions that may aggravate and worsen the situation, it's often possible to alleviate low-back pain and prevent it from becoming a chronic condition.

The mind-body connection in regard to back pain includes how you feel about your job. People who are unhappy at work because the job is unfulfilling or the pay is low tend to develop more back problems than the general population.

Other Risk Factors

How you live can make you more susceptible to back pain. Research shows that smokers are at greater risk. And being physically out of condition is one of the most common reasons why people have a recurrence of the sprain-and-strain type of back pain. I mention this again because I see many patients who are discouraged when a problem, which they thought was gone for good, comes back—often more than once.

Education also plays a role. People with more education have less low-back pain than others. This may be because with more education comes more leisure time, which can translate into more time available to devote to back-healthy, home-based or gym-based exercise. Less education may also be associated with heavy work and smoking, two risk factors I mentioned a moment ago.

If you recognize yourself in any of the risk categories I've described, it would be prudent to pay attention to why you are at risk and consider what changes you might make to your lifestyle or behaviors that could reduce your risk. Unfortunately, you can't do anything about your genes at this point, although scientists are working vigorously on how to compensate for genetic defects, such as an inherited tendency toward disk degeneration.

Your back is a complex machine with many parts. Understanding what these parts are and how they work together is imperative if you are to understand what happens when the machine malfunctions or underperforms. The next chapter explains just how it all works.

Part II

Understanding Back Pain

Chapter : 3

The Workings of Your Back

"Doctor, since February I've been having these bouts of back pain. I don't know why they keep coming back. It doesn't seem to be anything I'm doing and I can't seem to do anything to get rid of them." I hear comments like this weekly, if not more often. People with back pain naturally want to understand what's going on and what they can do about it. This isn't just curiosity for curiosity's sake. My patients want to be involved. Knowing what's going on makes them feel better. From my perspective, the more they know, the more favorably they'll respond to the management of their condition. And like my patients, you appreciate that knowledge is essential if you're to communicate effectively with your doctor and have some control over charting a course to a healthy back. Ultimately, you'll be the one making the decisions.

Often diagnosis and treatment of a long-lasting or chronic back problem require more than one approach targeted at a single aspect of your back. Instead, the problem—and hence the solution—may well relate to the interaction of several working parts and require several treatment approaches. But it's difficult to make sense of your back pain—and therefore how to relieve it—unless you understand something about the intricacies of how your back works.

This chapter has two parts. We begin with an explanation and description of the workings of the human back—the "big" back picture. Then we go on to look in detail at the five regions of the spine and their associated tissues.

The Wonder That Is Your Back

Your back is an extraordinary mechanical wonder. Consider how strong and reliable it must be to support all your day-to-day activities such as walking, running, and dancing. Yet, at the same time, your back must afford you the flexibility to bend and turn in all directions as you lift, garden, ski, and so on. But providing strength and flexibility are only part of what your back does. It has an even more crucial protective role: it encases the spinal cord and spinal nerve roots. These are critical information highways going to and from the brain, feet, arms, and so forth. Indeed, the bodywide network of nerves firing information back and forth is what makes us able to function. You need only think of the devastation wrought by a catastrophic horse riding accident that results in severe spinal cord injury and paralysis to appreciate how vital this protection is.

The marvel is not just what your back does overall, but how good it is at two seemingly contradictory tasks: providing protection against injury of the spinal cord and providing mobility for such activities as running, soccer, and picking up a small child. How does your back manage to do both? By becoming more knowledgeable about the workings of the spine and its accompanying tissues, we can understand why our backs are so good at what they do; why they occasionally experience a mechanical failure; and the ramifications of those failures. Let's start with a head to tail look at your back.

One way of thinking about the multifaceted back is like an elevator system in a busy, top-notch hotel. This analogy isn't as far-fetched as it might seem. First consider the hotel elevator system, an operation that comprises a sturdy, reinforced shaft within which motors and cables activate the up-and-down passage of the elevator. Access to this two-way thoroughfare is via elevator doors that open onto various floors, enabling a flow of traffic from all parts of the hotel. This system, which is coordinated by an elevator operation center, handles a lot of traffic: an assistant manager goes up from the lobby to a meeting on the fifth floor; guests go down to the exercise room in the basement; room service delivers meals from the kitchen to the tenth floor. This passage of people and products is essential to the functioning of the hotel. If any part of the elevator system is interrupted or is working below par, the smooth running of the entire hotel is affected.

Now consider your back and how it similarly facilitates the flow of information from all parts of your body and how this flow is coordinated by an operation center, your brain, encased in its hard hat of the skull. As with the hotel elevator system, your back has a number of different components, each one necessary for the smooth running of your body's traffic. The bony structure of your column-like spine protects the body's major electrical information conduit, the spinal cord, which lies snugly in the spinal canal. Joints, muscles, ligaments, and tendons are the auxiliary working parts—the motors, connectors, and cables that help ferry information up and down the spinal cord. Like the elevator doors that access the hotel floors, an arrangement in the bony structure of the spine (the intervertebral foramina) permits thirty-one pairs of nerve roots to connect the central nervous system (spinal cord and brain) with the rest of the body—the arms, legs, feet, and so on.

What matters in your body's system is the well-maintained, coordinated interaction of the parts. When the system has a mechanical or neurological failure, you soon know because of the pain you experience and your interrupted mobility.

Your Back's Equipment List

As you would expect, given the complexity of the workings of your back, a number of critical parts are involved. Because most back problems emanate from the cervical (neck) and lumbar (low-back) regions of the spine, we'll look at these two regions in some depth in this chapter and throughout the book. But before we take a close look at the anatomical specifics of those two locations, I'll introduce you to the various structures and the parts they play in the harmonious working of your back. Back problems can be caused by, or an existing problem exacerbated by, a malfunction of any of these structures and their relationships with one another.

Vertebrae. This is the name given to the unique, interlocking arrangement of bones that constitutes your spine. Bone, as you know, is the porous, calcified, hard connective tissue that makes up the skeleton of the body. Bones come in various shapes and sizes, with the spinal vertebrae being possibly the most distinctive. Like all bones, vertebrae are living tissue, and in common with other living tissues they contain blood vessels.

When you look at the human skeleton, you may wonder how something so seemingly rickety and frail does all the things it does. But bones are immensely strong. They can resist compression with strength equal to that of cast iron or oak. Although very light (the average adult human skeleton weighs a mere twenty pounds), bones are capable of bearing tremendous weight.

Be they in the spine or elsewhere in the body, bones protect and support internal organs. For instance, the canal formed by the

Turn, Turn, Turn

The interlocking bones of the spinal column called *vertebrae* got their name from the Latin term *vertere*, which means "to turn." Humans are vertebrates, meaning we belong to the subphylum Vertebrata. Conditions of membership include a segmented spinal column and a well-defined head. Those fishes, amphibians, reptiles, birds, and mammals that meet these criteria are also members of Vertebrata.

column-like arrangement of vertebral bones protects the spinal cord and its attendant nerve roots. Such protection, as I've mentioned, is extremely important since the spinal cord, together with the brain, constitutes the central nervous system, the information thoroughfare that is in direct, two-way communication with all the other nerves in the body.

Your vertebral spine also does a couple of very important things that are so obvious we take them for granted. One, it supports your head and stops it from falling onto your chest; two, it supports your entire weight against the constant pull of gravity.

I mentioned the distinctive shape of vertebrae. If you looked at your spine from the side, you'd see that individual vertebra are shaped rather like mini teapots minus their spouts. The forward facing part of the vertebra is slightly rounded. At the rear are bony protuberances reminiscent of handles. (Have a look at Figure 3.4 on page 46 and you'll see what I mean.)

Processes. This is the name of the arrangement of bony "handles" on the rear side of vertebrae that you can feel as bumps running down your back. In essence, processes function as handles to which muscles and tendons attach. Most vertebrae have seven processes, but this number can vary depending on which part of the spine you are looking at. The ones you can feel along your spine are called the *spinous processes*.

Intervertebral Disks. These disks consist primarily of cartilage, other connective tissue, and water. Functioning as joints, disks connect vertebrae to one another so that one vertebra can move relative to its neighbor. Positioned between individual vertebrae, the donut-shaped disks have gel-like centers called the *nucleus pulposus*, and a tougher outer covering called the *annulus fibrosus*.

Think of disks as tiny water beds. Their water-filled squishy interior allows the disks to change shape in response to pressure as the vertebrae move relative to one another. The cushioning effect disks provide prevents vertebrae from scraping against one another as they move. This accommodation happens every time you make a movement that involves your back—even when you are sitting in front of your computer and simply turn your head. In their role as the shock absorbers of the spine, disks afford your back protection from the bumps and bangs of you in motion.

Facet Joints. These joints are found in pairs and connect the back side of a vertebra to its neighboring vertebra via the processes. Similar to the connections between train cars, facet joints hook the vertebrae together while also allowing a controlled degree of movement between vertebrae. Cumulatively, the small movements each facet joint permits are what allow your spine to bend forward, backward, and to the side. These nifty joints are about the size of the knuckles of your little finger. To ensure the moving parts are kept well oiled, facets are contained within protective joint capsules filled with lubricating fluid called *synovial fluid*.

Muscles, Ligaments, and Tendons. These anatomical parts connect with vertebrae in various ways and make up the push-pull system that gives us such a remarkable range of motion. Consider the Houdini-like back bends of figure skaters or the amazing reach of tennis players as they lunge for match point.

In your body, most muscles are anchored to bone by tendons. When a muscle contracts, it pulls on the tendon, which in turn pulls on the bone. Ligaments connect bones to each other, which makes for stability. In that sense ligaments work like guy ropes keeping bony structures in place.

- **Muscles** typically work in groups. Movement is the coordinated action of a number of muscles responding to two-way signals between the brain and the muscle. Your brain directs the action of a muscle by sending a signal down the spinal cord to the nerve roots, which in turn transmit the signal to the muscles. Going the other way, special nerve endings inside the muscles send signals back to the spinal cord and on up to the brain. This relay system communicates moment-to-moment feedback to the operation center on the amount of tension in the muscles and tendons.

- **Tendons and ligaments** are made of connective tissue consisting of the proteins collagen and elastin. Collagen gives the tissue toughness and elastin gives it elasticity. The tendons and ligaments around the spine reinforce and stabilize the system of bones, joints, and muscles.

The combination of all the elements working harmoniously is what makes your back such a marvel of kinetic engineering. The elaborate interactions also explain why it's often impossible to pinpoint the precise cause of your back pain. Several different tissues may be injured, including muscle, nerve, tendon, vertebral bone, disk, facet joint, and others. It's not easy and often not possible to identify exactly which one or ones of these are responsible in a particular case.

Your Back Through the Ages

Although some people are born with abnormalities of the back, such as the distinctive spinal curvature of scoliosis or other congenital back problems, most of us are fortunately born with no major abnormalities. But as I've mentioned, the back is like a piece of machinery, and given how much use we routinely demand of our backs, it's not surprising that over time the machinery starts to show signs of wear and tear. Remarkably, though, for most of us, our backs age gracefully and we remain relatively pain free. However, the march of time does bring with it an increased risk of back conditions that result from degenerative processes occurring in the spine.

One common age-related back problem is the degeneration of disks that occurs in all of us over time. With age, biochemical changes in the disks cause them to lose water. As a result, disks become thinner, stiffer, and drier. Their squishy interior loses some of its squish. This diminishes the ability of disks to absorb shocks and makes the vertebrae and their facet joints more vulnerable to damage. If you have ever driven a car when its shock absorbers have gone, you get the picture. But don't think this is a problem for your dotage. Disks start to lose water from the age of thirty on.

Other degenerative back conditions that tend to appear later in life include spondylolisthesis (displacement of one vertebral bone with respect to the adjacent vertebra), osteoarthritis (degeneration of joint cartilage), and osteoporosis (thinning of the bone).

But with the exception of osteoporosis, which is related to age, these conditions aren't exclusively age-related. They can also result from injuries, such as athletic injuries, that occurred earlier in your life.

Although it's true that the risk of back problems increases as we age, on the whole, our backs serve us well and perform very reliably for as long as we need them. Now let's move on from the big picture of your back and consider your spine and its attributes in more detail.

Your Spine from Top to Bottom

Your spine is made up of thirty-three cylindrical, interlocking vertebrae (see Figure 3.1). The length of the spine is divided into five regions: the cervical spine (seven vertebrae), thoracic spine (twelve vertebrae), lumbar spine (five vertebrae), sacrum (five vertebrae), and coccyx (four vertebrae). Each vertebra within a region is uniquely named. These five regions vary greatly in flexibility, from no flexibility whatsoever (the sacrum) to very impressive flexibility (think of a ballerina's or figure skater's breathtaking twists and bends). The nine bottom vertebrae, which make up the sacrum and coccyx, are fused and immobile. The other vertebrae are not and provide the flexibility that enables you to bend, stretch, and lift. The cervical and lumbar spine are more flexible than the thoracic spine. Not surprisingly, the more mobile cervical and lumbar regions are where most back-pain problems originate. The wear and tear on the moving parts is the price we pay for flexibility.

Keeping the landscape and overall workings of the spine in mind, let's now look at the anatomical specifics of the cervical and lumbar spine regions.

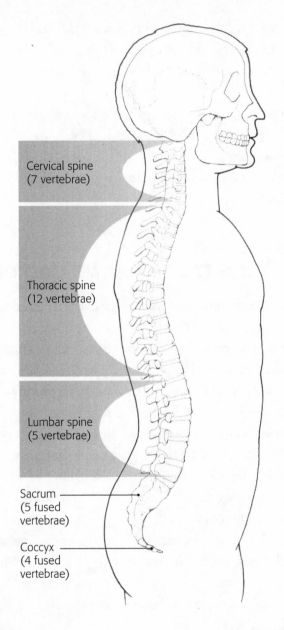

Cervical spine
(7 vertebrae)

Thoracic spine
(12 vertebrae)

Lumbar spine
(5 vertebrae)

Sacrum
(5 fused
vertebrae)

Coccyx
(4 fused
vertebrae)

Figure 3.1

Your Spine at a Glance

Your spine is divided into five regions, but most back pain is associated with
problems in the cervical and lumbar spine regions.

The Letters and Numbers System of Your Back

The individual vertebrae in your back are named for their location and their relative position at that location. The locations are the regions of the spine, identified by their first letters, and the numbers run from top to bottom. The first or top vertebra of the cervical spine is therefore C-1.

Not only does this simple, logical system identify the vertebrae, it also gives the coordinates of a problem stemming from a piece of your back's "equipment." For instance, your doctor may tell you your problem is degeneration of the disk between L-5 and S-1, meaning the culprit is the disk that separates the last vertebra of the lumbar spine from the first vertebra of the sacrum.

The Anatomy of Your Neck

Your neck's intricate scaffolding of bones and nerves provides support for your head and protection for your spinal column. But an area with so many interactions is ripe for problems. Bone may compress delicate nerves, joints can deteriorate, disks can bulge, and muscles and ligaments are liable to sustain injury through overuse. Muscle and ligament injury is the most common cause of neck pain.

The top seven vertebrae constitute the cervical spine. As well as protecting the spinal cord, the cervical spine has the distinctive responsibility of carrying and keeping steady the weight of your head, which tips the scale at about fifteen pounds. Like a movie camera, your head needs to make large movements and subtle adjustments in order to capture sights and sounds, but it won't work well if your head jerks when you move it. Similar to the award-winning camera design called the "Steadicam," the cervical spine supports the head with a curved, multipart structure capable of dampening sudden movements and preventing your head from jolting uncontrollably. The control and flexibility of these movements rely on the cervical spine's associated nerves, disks, muscles, ligaments, and tendons.

Neck Vertebrae. These vertebrae are named for their location. The first cervical vertebra, known as C-1, sits at the top of the spine, supporting the bottom of your skull. Many people can feel the seventh, the C-7 vertebra, as the prominent bump at the bottom of the neck. The great mobility of your neck is accomplished by adaptations to the interlocking vertebral pattern of especially the first two cervical vertebrae. The C-1 vertebra is named the *atlas*, after the Greek god Atlas who shouldered the weight of the world. Curves on the bottom of the occiput, the back section of your skull, fit into shallow grooves in the C-1 vertebra, forming the flexible joint that lets you nod your head "yes." Below C-1, the C-2 vertebra, called the *axis*, has an extension that sticks up through an opening in the atlas. This provides the pole around which your neck pivots as you shake your head "no." The C-3 through C-7 vertebrae aren't known by other names and are structured more like vertebrae in the lower spine. Each allows a relatively small amount of movement, but together they enable you to rotate or bend your head to the side and move it forward and backward (see Figure 3.2). But this mobility comes at a price. It can lead to injury and wear and tear. To understand this more we need to look at the various pieces of equipment that make up the moving whole.

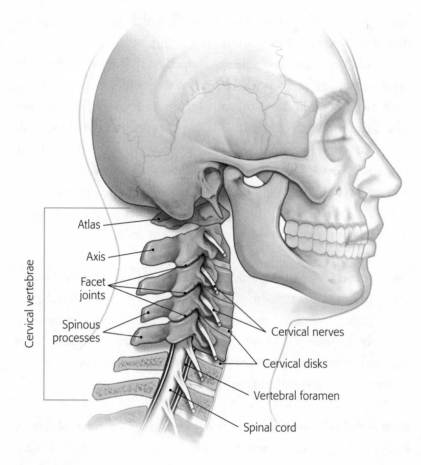

Figure 3.2

Where It Hurts: Bones and Nerves of the Neck

Your neck's complex architecture provides support for your head and protection for your spinal column.

Let's start with the interaction between the bony structures and the nerves of the spine.

Each cervical vertebra has a curved bony part in the front and a ring of bone attached to the back surrounding a hole called the *vertebral foramen* (plural: foramina). These holes line up to form the vertebral or spinal canal in which the spinal cord lies. A number of processes, or posterior elements, which project in several directions, are also found on the bony ring.

In addition, the vertebrae are shaped so that narrow openings on each side are created where each vertebra meets its upper and lower neighbors. These gaps, called the *intervertebral foramina*, are where the roots of eight pairs of spinal nerves exit the spinal column and extend to areas of your upper body. Although the bony structure provides excellent protection for the nerves, the space is tight, and the nerves sometimes become pinched between the bones. This causes pain in the neck, difficulty in movement, or sensation in the regions supplied by the nerves.

Facet Joints. These Lego-like connectors of the architecture of the spine are also rich in nerve endings. These can signal pain if the joint is squeezed or jerked past its normal range of motion, as might happen if you were involved in an auto accident. And like joints elsewhere in the body, facets are subject to degenerative damage from osteoarthritis.

Intervertebral Disks. These disks do a great job of cushioning individual vertebrae from one another, but over time, as I mentioned earlier, disks lose their cushion-like properties. This leads to all sorts of problems, which I talk about in Chapter 4.

Muscles. The muscles of your shoulders and upper back, particularly those between your shoulder blades, form an important base that supports your neck and head by keeping the cervical spine aligned properly, while at the same time allowing a great deal of movement. Of the two dozen or so large and small muscles in the neck and upper back, some have a single function, but most work in combinations enabling you to move in several directions. If you injure or overuse the muscles in your neck, you'll soon know. You'll hurt. Even sleeping in an awkward position or simply sitting at a desk all day can lead to muscle strain and pain. And muscle weakness in one or more muscle groups can make it difficult to maintain a healthy posture, which puts added stress on the disks and joints of the spine. In fact, being out of condition, or *deconditioned* as it's called, is an important risk factor for a return bout of the sprain-and-strain type of back pain. We'll be considering this in more detail later in the book.

At the back of your neck, wrapped around your shoulders like a shawl, are a group of posterior, or extensor, muscles that contract when you extend your neck. If you tend to stand, drive, and work at the computer with your head stuck out in front rather than directly balanced over your spine, your posterior neck muscles must stay contracted in order to keep your head upright. And that spells trouble. Although the muscles are quite strong, they can't withstand such prolonged effort and before too long may begin to ache. The trapezius muscle, which runs down the back of your neck and fans out toward your shoulders, is the largest of the extensor muscles (see Figure 3.3). If you feel a muscle knot in the back of your neck, typically halfway between the spine and the shoulder, the chances are it's in your trapezius.

Toward the front of the neck, your anterior, or flexor, muscles help balance and stabilize your head. These are the muscles you can feel working when you lie on your back and slightly lift your head off the floor (without tilting forward). Compared with the posterior muscles, the anterior muscles are relatively small and weak—particularly in people with neck pain.

Lateral muscles help balance your head and let you bend it to the side. Both the anterior and lateral muscles are easily overstretched and injured, such as in a whiplash-type accident when they readily tighten and cause neck pain.

Tendons and Ligaments. These are what hold everything together. Tendons are the strong flexible cords that attach the neck muscles to

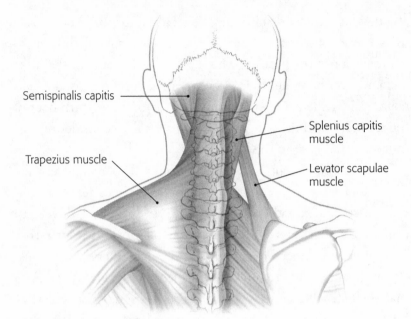

Semispinalis capitis

Trapezius muscle

Splenius capitis
muscle

Levator scapulae
muscle

Figure 3.3

Where It Hurts: Muscles of the Neck

The posterior (rear) neck muscles do the lion's share of the work of supporting
the weight of your head while it tilts and turns. Pain results when injury or overuse
strains or tears these neck muscles. The brawny trapezius muscle is one of the
most common sites of neck pain and strain.

bones, including the vertebrae of the cervical spine, collarbones, ribs,
shoulder blades, and skull. And the whole system of bones, joints,
and muscles is reinforced and stabilized by the ligaments, which
connect bones to one another and help prevent excessive movement that can cause damage. Ligaments come in varying lengths
with short ligaments connecting adjoining cervical vertebrae and
longer ligaments extending along the entire cervical spine.

Prepped with this understanding of the workings of the cervical spine, let's look at the comparable structures in the lumbar
spine.

The Anatomy of Your Lower Back

The lumbar spine, which consists of the lowest five mobile vertebrae of the spine, extends from the last vertebra of your thoracic spine (around the bottom of your rib cage) to your sacrum—the large triangular bone found between your hip bones. Your lumbar spine's strength and flexibility allow you to twist, turn, bend, stand, walk, run, and lift. It also supports most of your body's weight. This area of your spine is subjected to a great deal of stress when you perform your daily activities. For example, when you lift or carry heavy objects, extreme forces are being exerted on your lumbar spine. Not surprisingly, low-back pain, which comprises most cases of back pain, arises because of problems in the lumbar spine and its associated disks, nerves, muscles, ligaments, and tendons.

Vertebrae, Facet Joints, and Intervertebral Disks. These pieces of the lumbar spine work the same way as those of the cervical spine and are similarly vulnerable to overuse, injury, and degenerative damage (see Figure 3.4). I discuss the problems that can arise from this vulnerability in detail in Chapter 4.

There is, however, one major neuroanatomical difference between the cervical and lumbar spine. This is the arrangement of the spinal cord once it reaches the upper part of the lumbar spine. Up until this point, nerve roots have exited the spinal canal in pairs at each vertebra, like cars leaving a highway at specific exit ramps. At vertebra L-1, however, the spinal cord officially ends, becoming instead a bundle of nerve roots. Although some of the nerve roots continue to exit at each vertebral level, like in the higher part of the spine, the bundle of nerves continues downward in the lumbar spinal canal toward the sacrum. This bundle now resembles a horse's tail (see Figure 3.5), which is the origin of its name *cauda equina* (Latin for "horse's tail"). The cauda equina is an extremely sensitive aspect of spinal cord apparatus. The nerve

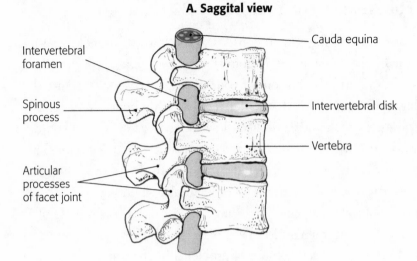

A. Saggital view

Intervertebral foramen

Spinous process

Articular processes of facet joint

Cauda equina

Intervertebral disk

Vertebra

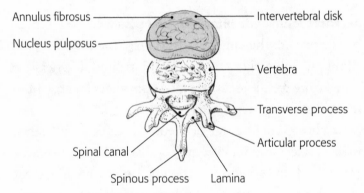

B. Cross-sectional view

Annulus fibrosus

Nucleus pulposus

Intervertebral disk

Vertebra

Transverse process

Articular process

Spinal canal

Spinous process   Lamina

Figure 3.4

A Closer Look at Your Lumbar Vertebrae

(A) Sagittal view: As in the cervical spine, each vertebra of the lumbar spine has a cylindrical body with a bony ring attached to its rear as well as processes that project out in different directions from this ring. Intervertebral disks, tucked between each pair of vertebrae, serve as shock absorbers. (B) Cross-sectional view: Each intervertebral disk has a squishy gelatinous center, the nucleus pulposus, and a tougher fibrous covering, the annulus fibrosus. In the lumbar spine each vertebra normally has seven stabilizing processes. Most cases of back pain emanate from the lumbar vertebrae and its associated parts.

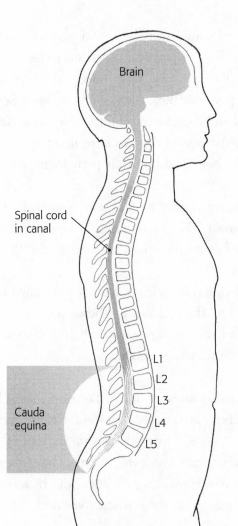

Figure 3.5

The Cauda Equina: A Horse's Tail of Nerve Roots

Your spinal cord runs from your brain down through your spinal column to end in the lumbar region. Nerve roots exit through two narrow channels, one on each side of adjacent vertebrae. But in the lumbar spine, the lowermost nerve roots become a bundle of nerve strands called the *cauda equina*—because the arrangement resembles a horse's tail.

fibers that control your leg muscles and play an important role in bladder, intestinal, and genital functions reside in these nerve roots. Similarly, your sensory nerve fibers, which provide feeling from your toes up to your hips, travel via these same nerve roots to your spinal cord and then to your brain. You can understand why suspected nerve damage to the cauda equina requires immediate action to prevent serious and possibly permanent damage.

Muscles. The interaction of musculature is essential to the functionality of the low back. Three muscle groups supply support and flexibility to the lumbar spine (see Figure 3.6):

- The flat **abdominal muscles** in front are attached to the pelvis below and the ribs above. These muscles, which form the cavity that contains your stomach and other abdominal organs, also support your lumbar spine.

- The two **iliopsoas muscles**, located one on each side of your lumbar vertebrae, are attached to the vertebrae and to the inside of your pelvis. Passing downward in front of your hip joints and attaching to your thighbones, these muscles not only support your spine, they also flex your hips and help balance your trunk on your legs when you stand.

- The **erector spinae**, which are located to the left and right of your spine in the rear, are the large muscle masses you can see in the lower part of your back. They are composed of many muscle groups attached to the bony processes on each vertebra, as well as to the pelvis below and the rib cage and thoracic and cervical regions of the spine above. *Erector spinae* is Latin for "upholder of the spine," and these muscles are the major supports of your spine when you lift things.

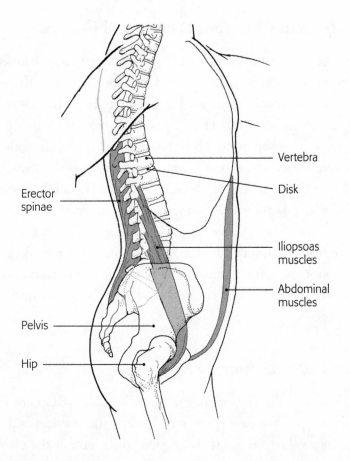

Vertebra

Disk

Erector spinae

Iliopsoas muscles

Abdominal muscles

Pelvis

Hip

Figure 3.6

The Supporting Muscles of the Lumbar Spine

Three groups of muscles—the erector spinae, abdominal muscles, and iliopsoas muscles—support your spine and control low-back movements. The abdominal muscles also form your abdominal cavity, and the iliopsoas muscles allow you to flex your hips and help balance your trunk when you're standing.

We've looked in some detail at the workings of the cervical and lumbar spine, the two regions of your spine that are most likely to have problems. But the other three regions—the thoracic spine, sacrum, and coccyx—are vulnerable, too.

The Bottom Bits: Your Sacrum and Coccyx

Your sacrum, the wedge-shaped bone in your pelvis, is connected to the lumbar spine at the top end and the coccyx at the lower end. It carries much of the load of the upper body. In most adults the sacrum consists of five fused vertebrae. But the sacrum is also the region of the spine that has the most individual variability.

Interestingly, when we are born the vertebrae of the sacrum are similar to the vertebrae of the lumbar spine. The adult sacrum as we know it isn't fully fused until we are between twenty-five and thirty years of age. Your coccyx, sometimes called the *tailbone*, is precisely that—four fused vertebrae that in our evolutionary ancestors were a functioning tail. Both the sacrum and coccyx are vulnerable to fractures from accidents or the bone thinning of osteoporosis.

Your Thoracic Spine

Your thoracic spine has more vertebrae—twelve—than any other region of the spine and is located between the cervical and lumbar spine. Why have I left this region to the end of the chapter? Because it has the least problems. The reason? Your ribs, which lend the thoracic spine stability and help minimize wear and tear. Your thoracic spine isn't invulnerable, however. As you age, it's the prime location of the fractures associated with osteoporosis.

Enough with the Anatomy!

The anatomy of the back is a lot to digest in a single read. Even most medical school students would agree with that! But in the treatment of back pain, especially if you're considering surgery, understanding the basics of back anatomy is important. You may want to return to this chapter at a later date to check out a detail. Now let's move on to a discussion of why bad things happen to good backs, a review of the more common types of back-pain problems.

Chapter 4

Why Your Back Hurts

Back pain is not a disease per se, but rather the body's way of notifying you about an injury or underlying back condition. Consequently, the causes of back pain are many. The three that head the list are sprain-and-strain injuries, pinched nerve syndromes, and vertebral osteoporotic fractures. But you shouldn't rule out inflammation, infection, arthritis, and trauma. Tumor is another possibility, although far less likely.

In this chapter I'll be taking you through these back conditions and their more common symptoms in some detail. Before we start, though, to give you a sense of how all this may apply to you, Table 4.1. shows when in your life you're more likely to be affected by certain types of back problems.

Your spine is a large landscape divided into a number of different regions. From this point on we'll be focusing on problems that can arise in the cervical and lumbar regions of the spine. For the most part, the causes of back pain discussed in this chapter are common to both the cervical and lumbar spine. To avoid repetition, when I refer to conditions of the spine in this chapter, I'm referring to conditions that affect both these regions of the back

Table 4.1

Frequency and Risk of Back Conditions

Category	Condition	
Sprain-and-strain syndromes	Injury to muscles and ligaments	
Pinched nerve syndromes	**In the Lumbar Spine**	
	Herniated disk (sciatica)	
	Lumbar spinal stenosis	
	Spondylolisthesis (often accompanied by spondylolysis)	
	Cauda equina syndrome	
	In the Cervical Spine	
	Cervical radiculopathy (nerve root compression)	
	Cervical myelopathy (spinal cord compression)	
Degenerative spinal disease	Osteoarthritis of the facet joints	

Common Symptoms	Frequency and Risk
Acute pain that includes stiffness and muscle spasms; limited range of motion; tension headache if the problem is in the cervical spine (whiplash, for example)	Most common type of back pain; can occur at any age; will heal without medical intervention, but frequently recurs
A sharp constant or shooting pain along the sciatic nerve	Peak incidence 30–50 years of age
Pain in the lower back, possibly radiating down one or both legs; leg weakness; poor balance; falls (rare); urinary frequency (rare)	Two forms: congenital or acquired. Congenital affects people in their 30s and 40s; acquired is more common after 60 years of age
Low-back pain; discomfort in thighs and hips; maybe sciatica in both legs. Many people have no symptoms	Two forms: congenital and acquired. Congenital appears in childhood; acquired over 50 years of age and affects more women than men. Also affects athletes
Weakness of the legs, disturbances of bladder and bowel function, "saddle anesthesia"	A rare surgical emergency; can occur in patients with large disk herniations, severe stenosis, infections, and tumors
Pain in the arms and hands	Conditions of the cervical spine are analogous to but less common than their counterparts in the lumbar spine (the lumbar spine has twice the reported number of back problems compared to the cervical spine)
Difficulty with coordination and gait	
Intermittent or chronic stiffness and pain similar to that of sprain and strain	Most common in later years; affects women more than men

(continued)

Table 4.1

Frequency and Risk of Back Conditions continued

Category	Condition	
Fractures	Osteoporosis (vertebral fractures)	
	Spondylolysis	
Infection	Diskitis (disks) Osteomyelitis (vertebrae) Infectious arthritis (facet joints)	
Inflammation	Inflammatory spinal arthritis: ankylosing spondylitis	
Unknown causes	Fibromyalgia syndrome	
	Myofascial pain syndrome	
	Scoliosis (several causes including inborn and idiopathic)	
Trauma	Severe injury Fracture	
Tumor	Usually metastatic, the cancer originating elsewhere in the body (typically in the breast, lung, or prostate)	

Common Symptoms	Frequency and Risk
Sudden severe pain in the area of the fracture that lessens as the fracture heals	Most common in postmenopausal women
Low-back pain; may include the numbness and tingling of sciatica	Any age; due to overuse injuries (athletes), degenerative change (the elderly), or inherited tendency
Fever, severe pain or tenderness around the affected vertebrae, possible muscle spasms	Rare emergency conditions that can occur at any age
Pain, stiffness, and loss of motion	A chronic rheumatic condition that affects adolescents and young men (aged 15–30 years) more than women
Muscle, ligament, and tendon pain; tender points painful to the slightest touch; morning stiffness; headache; numbness and tingling in the hands and feet; cognitive and sleep difficulties	Typically occurs in middle-aged women, although men and children can also have it; second most common condition seen by rheumatologists
Muscle pain; stiffness, limited range of motion; referred pain from trigger points	Very common; occurs at any age
Usually painless, but surrounding muscles can become strained and painful	Most frequently diagnosed in early adolescence
Signs of neurological damage	Occurs at any age; a rare emergency
Severe, dull, relentless pain	Can occur at any age

unless I specify otherwise. Note that some conditions are named differently when they occur in the cervical and lumbar spine.

Keeping all this in mind, let's now look at the causes of back pain in detail.

Sprain-and-Strain Syndromes

Soft-tissue damage of the muscles, ligaments, and tendons important for movement and support is the most common reason for back pain. Given the amount of musculature and associated ligaments and tendons in the cervical and lumbar regions of the spine and the constant push and pull they engage in, you can appreciate why sprain and strain of these tissues is the number one cause of problems in both regions. In days gone by, you'd sometimes hear sprain and strain referred to as "lumbago."

The terms "sprain" and "strain" indicate which tissues are involved. Strain refers to muscle injury and results when tissues

A Touch of Lumbago

Perhaps you recall an elderly relative complaining of having a "touch of lumbago," meaning he or she was bedeviled with nagging back pain. *Lumbago*, a term seldom used today, was once commonly used to describe low-back pain and, by association, any type of sprain and strain of the back. It comes from the Latin word lumbus, meaning loin. Lumbus is the root word for lumbago and lumbar, as in "lumbar back."

overstretch or sustain microscopic tears. Repeated overuse or a single injury or overexertion can cause damage—often referred to as a "pulled" muscle. If the stretching and tearing occur in a ligament rather than a muscle, the injury is called a *sprain*. Sprains are typically caused by extreme bends or an awkward twist.

Although episodes of sprain and strain can result from trauma, such as whiplash following a car accident or sports-related injuries, most episodes occur when we go about our daily routines. For instance, the seemingly mundane activities of lifting a heavy object, such as hoisting a heavy suitcase, or twisting and bending awkwardly when standing or sitting are all activities that can hurt the soft tissues of your neck and lower back. Holding your head in an uncomfortable position for some time as you paint the living room ceiling will also do it. Sometimes you don't have to do anything at all to end up in pain. An example is sleeping in a poor position that doesn't healthily support your neck, such as when you sleep on your stomach with your head twisted to one side.

Episodes of sprain and strain may be painful in the short-term, but for most people the problem will become less painful in a matter of days and completely clear up in several weeks without the need for professional medical intervention. That's the good news; the bad news is there's the likelihood of a repeat episode within six months for about 40 percent of us. But this discouraging prognosis can be avoided. Research has shown that exercise focused on strengthening the back and legs can reduce the number of recurrences of back pain. If you've recently had a sprain-and-strain back problem that has further encouraged your couch potato habits, the clock is ticking. It's time to dust off those well-intentioned resolutions of getting back in shape that failed to materialize!

Symptoms of sprain-and-strain syndrome are pain, which can be severe at the onset, but should progressively lessen over a period of days or weeks; stiffness and muscle spasms (muscle contractions); reduced ability to move in one or more directions; possibly

What Is Whiplash?

Whiplash describes both a group of symptoms and the type of accident that causes neck pain. The classic setup for whiplash is when you're rear-ended in a car accident and your head jerks back and then snaps forward. In medical parlance, whiplash is a hyperextension or acceleration-deceleration injury. It's not limited to car accidents; it can happen when riding a roller coaster or if you get punched in the face.

The force of a whiplash injury typically causes the muscles of the neck to strain and ligaments to stretch or tear. Whiplash symptoms include pain aggravated by movement; worsening pain in the days following the accident as the tissues swell; shoulder pain; muscle spasms in the neck or upper shoulders; stiffness and decreased range of motion; headache; tingling or weakness in the arms; and sometimes irritability, fatigue, sleep difficulties, or poor concentration.

The damage should heal within a few months, but some people experience lingering pain and other symptoms, which they should check out with their doctor in case there are additional injuries to the facet joints and disks.

some swelling of the affected area; and tension headache if the problem is in the cervical spine region. The symptoms are typically confined to the back, without pain radiating to the legs (lumbar sprain and strain) or the arms (cervical sprain and strain). The pain may feel "sharp" or "achy." The symptoms of sprain and strain don't include numbness or tingling. Those are the telltale symptoms of nerve root compression as you'll see in the section on pinched (compressed) nerve syndromes coming up soon.

Fibromyalgia Syndrome

I'm including fibromyalgia here because although not strictly speaking a "pure" back problem, the tender points that distinguish fibromyalgia from other conditions tend to occur in the muscles of the upper neck and shoulders, and the lower back and hips—as well as elsewhere in the body. The name fibromyalgia comes from the Latin term for fibrous tissue (*fibro*) and the Greek terms for muscle (*myo*) and pain (*algia*).

Fibromyalgia, which is the second most common disorder seen by rheumatologists, is a syndrome rather than a single condition. As a syndrome, fibromyalgia is a collection of symptoms and medical problems that can happen at the same time, but which are not related to one identifiable cause. This makes fibromyalgia difficult to diagnose and even more difficult to treat. People with certain rheumatic diseases, such as rheumatoid arthritis, systemic lupus erythematosus (lupus), or ankylosing spondylitis (spinal arthritis) may be more prone to have fibromyalgia. Overall, women are hardest hit, being seven times more likely to develop the condition than men.

The pain associated with fibromyalgia may result from changes in the central nervous system that cause the pain system to stay "switched on," leading to heightened, ongoing pain. The reason for these changes is unknown. Some experts speculate that a powerful pain impulse from the body or nerve impulses sent over and over again physically change the central nervous system. Levels of pain-sensing neurotransmitters rise and nerve cells become altered so they are more easily "excited" by pain signals. (I talk about this phenomenon in Chapter 6.) They may even process normal touch sensations as if they were pain impulses.

Symptoms of fibromyalgia syndrome are chronic widespread pain; painful tender points, which are sore to the touch with even a slight pressure; fatigue; stiffness upon awakening; sleep problems; and a host of other symptoms that may include headache, numbness and tingling of the extremities, restless leg syndrome, and more. Sometimes patients have "fibro fog," which refers to memory and cognitive problems. The syndrome can be difficult to diagnose and initially can be mistaken for sprain-and-strain syndrome.

Myofascial Pain Syndrome

The fascia is comprised of uninterrupted sheets of fibrous connective tissue that wrap around every muscle, bone, nerve, blood vessel, and organ of the body helping these structures stay in place. For reasons unknown, sensitive, painful spots, so-called "trigger points," develop where muscle and fascia meet, hence the name "myofascial." Many things can cause trigger points including injury to muscles, ligaments, tendons, and intervertebral disks. Tension and stress are implicated, as are fatigue, excessive exercise, repetitive motions, hormonal changes, and nutritional deficiencies. Many patients who have myofascial pain syndrome also have fibromyalgia.

Myofascial pain syndrome is difficult to diagnose. Some doctors think this little understood condition is an often-overlooked cause of back pain. Other doctors don't believe the condition exists. My take is that the notion of myofascial pain is useful. I see a number of patients with muscular pain, tenderness, and trigger points. They often respond to heat, massage, stress reduction, and improvements in posture.

Symptoms of myofascial pain syndrome are painful trigger points, which are distinguished by a taut thickening of the muscle. The pain, though, may be felt elsewhere, known as "referred" pain. Shortness of breath may be associated with neck pain.

Pinched (Compressed) Nerve Syndromes

Pinched nerve disorders include a number of painful back conditions, particularly sciatica. These disorders are major causes of back pain, especially in younger persons. Unlike the muscle and ligament pain of sprain and strain, the pain here is the result of pressure on nerves—either the peripheral nerve roots or the spinal cord. The resultant pain, caused by damaged and inflamed nerves, is different from soft-tissue pain. This distinction is important because it determines which diagnostic and treatment approaches will be more effective.

Degenerative conditions of vertebrae, facet joints, and disks are the major culprits in this category. As the structures of the back age, they change. Osteophytes, or bone spurs, may develop; disks narrow and may bulge out; and the ligaments of the spine and spinal canal may thicken. These changes may lead to a compression or "pinching" of nerve roots, the peripheral nerves that connect to the spinal cord. Sometimes the pain is due to a narrowing (stenosis) of the spinal column itself, which can lead to compression of peripheral nerves or the spinal cord, depending on where the narrowing occurs.

Degenerative Disk Conditions

Degenerative disk disease develops gradually over time as the shock-absorbing disks between the vertebrae shrink and become less flexible. But remember, this degenerative process starts relatively early in life with disk problems occurring when people are in their thirties, forties, and fifties. It's important then not to associate degenerative disk disease with old age and assume back pain is an inevitable aspect of aging. It isn't.

Herniated Disk

This refers to a displacement of some portion of the intervertebral disk from its normal position. As we age our disks tend to dry out. A brittle disk that has lost its water-bed-like properties becomes subject to a lot of pressure from its surrounding vertebrae. The combination of this pressure and the drying out of the tougher, outer annulus layer of the disk can cause the disk to tear in such a way that its gel-like center, the nucleus pulposus, bulges through the fibrous annulus. This bulge can "pinch" or put severe pressure on nerve roots. It can also protrude into the spinal canal and cause compression of the spinal cord (in the cervical spine) or the cauda equina (in the lumbar spine). Medical terms for this problem include disk *protrusion*, disk *herniation*, or disk *bulge*. You'll also see it referred to as a "ruptured" or a "slipped" disk.

Sciatica

Pain emanating from the sciatic nerves is the main symptom of a herniated disk. Sometimes referred to as a "trapped nerve," sciatica is most common in people aged forty to sixty. Sciatica can also be brought on by spinal stenosis, infection, fractures of the pelvis or thigh, or a tumor.

Symptoms of sciatica (herniated disk) are a sharp pain that runs along the course of the sciatic nerve, the long nerve in the body that passes through the buttock, down the back of the leg, and into the foot (see Figure 4.1). There are two sciatic nerves—one for each leg. Sciatic pain is often accompanied by a "pins and needles" sensation in the affected leg, especially in the foot and toes. The symptoms worsen with movement, assuming certain positions, coughing, sneezing, or doing anything that pulls on the sciatic nerve, such as bending forward from your waist or flexing your hips while keeping your knees straight. Sciatic pain comes in

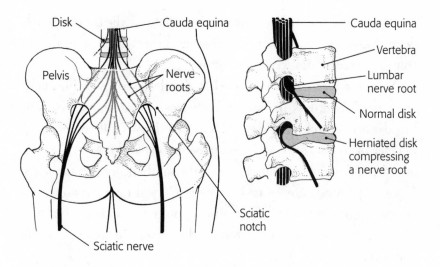

Figure 4.1

Causes of Sciatica

The cauda equina starts at vertebra L-1 where the end of the spinal cord branches into nerve roots. Four of these roots thread throughout the pelvis and merge to form the sciatic nerves, the longest nerves in the body, that extend down each leg. In the most common form of sciatica, a herniated disk squeezes a sciatic nerve root against the backbone, causing inflammation and pain. Sciatica can also be brought on by spinal stenosis, infection, fractures of the pelvis or thigh, or tumor.

two flavors: constant or shooting. The condition is so painful that people will do what they can to limit their movements. When the pain is constant, it's difficult to find a comfortable position; when it's occasional, sharp, and shooting, it feels like an electric shock.

Cauda Equina Syndrome

This serious condition is caused by large, central disk herniation or spinal stenosis in the lumbar region that compresses several nerves in the cauda equina. It can also be caused by rare problems such as tumor or infection. Cauda equina syndrome is a red flag, or emergency, situation requiring immediate medical help. If you delay seeking medical help, you risk permanent damage to nerves that govern essential body functions.

Symptoms of cauda equina that should set off warning bells are severe weakness in one or both legs; a disturbance of your bladder and bowel functions, such as inability to fully empty your bladder or to control your bowel movements; and possibly "saddle anesthesia," which is a numbness in the anal and/or genital areas. If you experience any of these symptoms, you may require emergency diagnostic tests to determine if you have cauda equina syndrome. If you do, surgery is often needed to relieve pressure on the trapped nerves.

Spinal Stenosis

Stenosis means narrowing. A number of degenerative changes can cause narrowing of the spinal column in which the spinal cord lies; or narrowing of the intervertebral foramina, the bony gaps through which the nerve roots exit the spinal column and extend to other areas of the body.

Space is quite tight in the spinal column and foramina. It doesn't take much change to pinch or damage the spinal cord or nerve roots (see Figure 4.2). A herniated disk or osteophytes (bone spurs) can protrude into the spinal column; ligaments can become enlarged or displaced; and the vertebra's bony plate (the lamina) can thicken. Since age-related degenerative conditions are often the cause of the problem, spinal stenosis most commonly affects people over fifty years of age. In some instances, people have an inborn anatomical propensity for spinal stenosis; and in very rare instances, it's the result of an unusual disease, such as Paget's disease, a condition in which bones enlarge and weaken.

Symptoms of lumbar spinal stenosis are pain aggravated by activity and bending backward at the waist and relieved by bend-

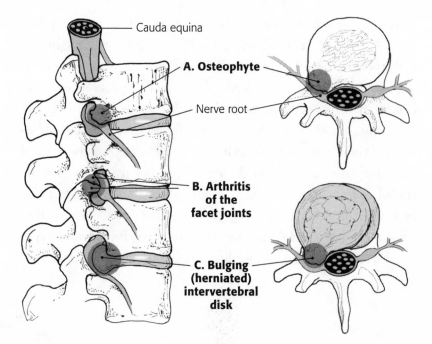

Cauda equina

A. Osteophyte

Nerve root

B. Arthritis of the facet joints

C. Bulging (herniated) intervertebral disk

Figure 4.2

An Example of the Pinched Nerve Syndrome: Compression of Nerve Roots

Nerve roots can be painfully compressed in several ways. Among the various causes of compression are: (A) an osteophyte or bone spur, (B) arthritis of the facet joints, and (C) a herniated—or bulging—intervertebral disk.

ing forward. Lumbar stenosis is also characterized by pain radiating down one or both legs, leg weakness, and, rarely, urinary frequency and falls. In some cases there are no obvious symptoms. In the cervical spine, stenosis goes under different names depending on the type of compression.

Spondylolisthesis

This term describes the slippage of one vertebra over another. In younger persons it occurs when a defect in the bony posterior elements of one vertebra permits the front portion of that vertebra, as well as the vertebra above it, to slip forward out of alignment with the spine. (See also "Spondylolysis" below.) In older persons degenerative changes can lead to instability and slippage. This condition takes its name from the Greek words for spine (*spondylo*) and slipping (*listhesis*). It's also referred to as *forward subluxation* of the vertebra. The condition can be caused by the gradual wear and tear of aging on the structures, but it isn't necessarily age related. It can also result from injury, repeated small fractures, or it may be inborn. In the general population, spondylolisthesis is more common in women than in men. But certain types of athletes—including weight lifters, football players (particularly

Differences in Nomenclature of Neck and Low-Back-Pain Disorders

Several pinched nerve syndromes are distinctly named to identify the regions of the back they affect. The conditions don't essentially differ between the neck and low back—only their names are different. In the cervical spine they are called:

- **Cervical radiculopathy**, which describes compression of the nerve root of the cervical spine. It can result from a herniated disk, spinal stenosis, or degenerative disk disease. Symptoms are generally pain in the arms and hands, often accompanied with numbness and tingling.

- **Cervical myelopathy**, which is a condition resulting from pressure on the cervical spinal cord or its blood vessels. It can be caused by inborn narrowing of the spinal column, spinal stenosis, bone spurs, a herniated disk protruding into the spinal column, or enlarged ligaments. In rare cases, it is caused by an infection or tumor. Symptoms are difficulty with coordination and gait, but not necessarily arm pain. Urinary incontinence may occur in severe cases.

One way to distinguish between the two cervical conditions is to think of nerve roots as feeder roads to the main highway of the spinal cord. But just as a buildup of traffic on feeder roads and highways impedes traffic flow and makes for a miserable commute, so, too, cervical radiculopathy and cervical myelopathy, which are often found together in the same person, make for a miserable upper back problem.

In the lumbar spine, stenosis is usually referred to as *lumbar spinal stenosis*. The stenosis results in compression of the nerve roots of the cauda equina, since, as you recall from Chapter 3, the cord ends at L-1 and the bundle of nerves is thereafter called the *cauda equina*.

• •

linemen), gymnasts, and sumo wrestlers—are especially prone to the defect in the bony posterior elements that leads to this condition. People with diabetes have four times the average risk for this problem and it's more common in women. Although it can occur in the neck, spondylolisthesis is more commonly seen in the lower back.

Symptoms of spondylolisthesis include low-back pain and discomfort in the thighs and hips. You may also experience sciatica, often in both legs. Many persons with spondylolisthesis, though, do not have symptoms.

Spondylolysis

This is the fracture of a small area of bone—the pars interarticularis—that connects the rounded front part of the vertebra. (Remember the teapot analogy in Chapter 3?) These tiny fractures may occur as the result of injury, overuse (as in athletes), degenerative weakening (as in elderly), or perhaps an inherited tendency. Spondylolysis is often found together with spondylolisthesis because the pars fracture permits the vertebral bones to slip with respect to one another.

Symptoms of spondylolysis are typically back pain and radiating pain in the legs, often with numbness or tingling (sciatica). These are also the symptoms of spondylolisthesis because the two conditions often occur together.

Degenerative Spinal Disease

Spinal structures change over time, which can lead to back-pain problems for some people as they age. Degenerative osteoarthritis of the spine, as with osteoarthritis in other parts of the body, is more common among older people. In osteoarthritis of the spine, the cartilage in the facet joints connecting the vertebrae gradually breaks down. Cartilage is connective tissue that cushions the end of the bones and reduces the friction between bones as joints move. Progressive osteoarthritis, with its signature symptoms of stiffness and pain, causes the bones to begin to grind on themselves. Over time, the vertebrae change shape and develop small bone spurs called *osteophytes*, which can compress nerves and cause pain.

Symptoms of degenerative osteoarthritis are stiffness and pain, which can be intermittent or chronic. The symptoms are located typically in the central low-back area without radiation into the legs. There is sometimes radiation of pain into the buttocks. This pattern resembles that of sprain and strain, which is why, as I mentioned in the first chapter of the book, these entities can be hard to distinguish and doctors consider them together in terms of treatment regimens.

Degenerative arthritis may lead to lumbar spinal stenosis. Osteophytes in the facet joints may compress the spinal nerve roots. In these cases the patient will experience the symptoms of spinal stenosis, which I described earlier in this chapter. In this situation, spinal stenosis is caused by the narrowing effect of osteopyhytes on the structures of the spine.

Other Causes of Back Pain

A number of other causes, such as congenital conditions, degenerative vertebral disease, inflammatory arthritis, infection, trauma, tumor, inborn conditions, and even unrelated disorders can cause . back pain. Although less common than sprain and strain or pinched nerve syndromes, nonetheless, you should not rule out the possibility that one of these disorders may be responsible for your backache. And it's very important that you move swiftly if you think the back pain you're experiencing may be an indication of a "red flag" condition.

Recognizing Red Flag Situations

For most back problems, not only can you afford to wait before seeking medical procedures, but waiting is usually the initial medical recommendation because in many cases backs will heal themselves. There are, however, a number of situations when not only should you not wait, but you should seek medical help right away. These conditions, such as cauda equina syndrome, trauma, infec-

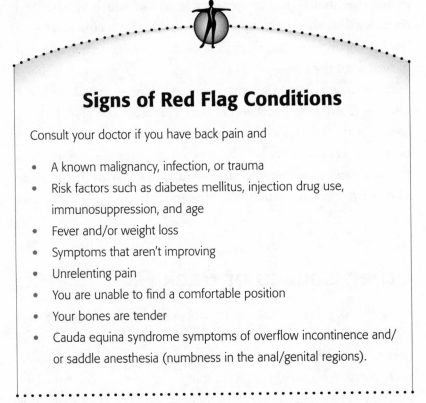

Signs of Red Flag Conditions

Consult your doctor if you have back pain and

- A known malignancy, infection, or trauma
- Risk factors such as diabetes mellitus, injection drug use, immunosuppression, and age
- Fever and/or weight loss
- Symptoms that aren't improving
- Unrelenting pain
- You are unable to find a comfortable position
- Your bones are tender
- Cauda equina syndrome symptoms of overflow incontinence and/ or saddle anesthesia (numbness in the anal/genital regions).

tion, or tumor, are potentially very serious and require prompt action. Fortunately, they are rare.

Scoliosis

Scoliosis, an abnormal sideways curvature and tilting of the spine, doesn't fit neatly into a single causal category of back pain. It can be caused by congenital defects, or muscle weakness or poor muscle control because of another disease such as cerebral palsy, muscular dystrophy, spina bifida, or polio. Often, however, the cause is unknown (idiopathic). The disorder, which typically isn't noticeable until a growth spurt during adolescence, is usually painless.

As it slowly progresses, an S-shaped curvature may develop in the spine as the body compensates for the original curvature. In mild cases, where there is only a small curve, no treatment is necessary. For more severe cases, your doctor may recommend an immobilizing brace. The spinal vertebrae can also be realigned and fused together using surgery to straighten the spine.

Symptoms of scoliosis are variable. The curve per se does not cause symptoms unless it is pronounced enough to cause the bottom ribs to rub against the brim of the pelvis. However, the muscles of the back, especially the trapezius and rhomboids, may become chronically fatigued, strained, and painful from constantly maintaining a neutral posture despite the intrinsic curve in the spine.

Osteoporosis

Osteoporosis is a degenerative, bone-thinning disease that is found in postmenopausal women whose bones can become weaker, more porous, and more susceptible to fracture over time. Men can develop osteoporosis, too, but the condition generally occurs earlier and more often in women. Although more common in the vertebrae, osteoporotic fractures are not limited to the spine. They can occur in the hips, wrist, and upper arms, as well as other locations. In the United States, osteoporosis causes 750,000 compression fractures each year. When the condition occurs in the spine, one or more vertebrae can collapse, causing a loss of height and a curvature of the spine. This distinctive rounding of the back is commonly known as a "dowager's hump"; the medical term is *kyphosis* (see Figure 4.3).

In persons with severe osteoporosis, painful compression fractures can result from something as innocuous as sneezing or lifting a gallon of milk. As many as two-thirds of vertebral compression fractions go undiagnosed in the United States. The attendant pain is attributed to back pain of an unknown (idiopathic) cause.

Fractured vertebrae in the thoracic region of the spine can lead to kyphosis, the medical term for a humped back.

Wedge fractures are a type of vertebral fracture. The front edge of the bone collapses more than the back edge, so the spine bends forward.

Figure 4.3

Osteoporotic Fracture of the Spine

Osteoporotic fractures are more common in older women.

The major symptom of osteoporotic compression fractures is severe and disabling back pain that comes on suddenly. The pain tends to be localized in the region of the affected vertebra, but it may radiate around one or both sides of your trunk. Movement increases pain and lying down usually relieves or at least improves it.

Inflammatory Arthritis of the Spine

This is a category that includes a number of conditions. As well as the ravages of the degenerative joint process, the arthritic inflammatory process gives rise to a group of poorly understood, interrelated inflammatory disorders that affect the spinal ligaments. In these diseases ligament can be converted to bone, resulting in pain and loss of motion. Ankylosing spondylitis is the most common of these inflammatory diseases.

Ankylosing Spondylitis

This condition gets its name from the Greek word *ankylos* meaning bent, and *spondylos* meaning vertebra, and is a condition in which the spine becomes inflamed and stiffens. In severe cases, over time the vertebral joints spontaneously fuse and the back becomes completely rigid. The disease, which usually begins before age forty, is more common and more severe in men. A mild case can be misdiagnosed as a sprain or strain or intervertebral disk problem.

Symptoms of ankylosing spondylitis are diminished flexibility and increasing pain over time. Sometimes the pain is on both sides of the lower back or pelvis.

Bacterial Infections of the Spine

Infections of the spine involving a disk (diskitis), one or more vertebrae (osteomyelitis), or the facet joints (infectious arthritis) are rare but do occur. Bacteria reach the spine from other sites via the bloodstream. The source might be a boil or another skin infection, a urinary tract infection, an abscessed tooth, or an unsterilized hypodermic needle. You're more likely to develop a spinal infection if your immune system is already compromised in one way or another, for example, by liver failure, conditions such as diabetes, HIV infection, or AIDS, or medications that interfere with your immune system, such as steroids or cancer-fighting drugs.

Symptoms of back infections are severe pain, fever, tenderness around the infected vertebrae, and possibly muscle spasms.

Trauma

Injuries, such as a car injury or a fall from a ladder, are potentially very serious. If you suspect that trauma has done damage to the back, call emergency services. Do *not* attempt to move the person and risk severely damaging the spinal cord.

Tumors

Tumors are fortunately rare causes of back pain, but they do occur. And whether they are malignant or benign, they can be quite painful. Most spinal tumors develop after the spread (metastasis) of a cancer that originated elsewhere, especially in the breast, lung, or prostate gland. Primary tumors can also arise in the bones, ligaments, spinal cord, or nerve roots.

Depending on its location, a spinal tumor can be confused, at least for a time, with almost any category of back pain, including sprain and strain, nerve compression (herniated disk), or fracture. But the treatment approaches that alleviate the pain of the common categories of backache tend not to be helpful for tumor pain. Because tumors are relatively rare and their symptoms similar to other back conditions, the correct tumor diagnosis is often delayed.

Symptoms of tumor mimic the symptoms of other causes of back pain, but the pain and discomfort caused by a tumor is usually constant and progressive.

Backache from Other Organs

Some causes of backache don't originate in your back. In these cases, the back pain you feel is what is called "referred" pain, meaning it comes from another part of the body yet you feel it in your back. Disorders of various abdominal and pelvic organs—including the pancreas, kidneys, or uterus—can cause back pain. An aneurysm of your aorta (a ballooning of the vessel wall), the large blood vessel that carries blood from your heart to your lower trunk and legs, can also cause back pain.

Symptoms vary and may mimic more common types of back pain. If movements and activities you might expect would stress the spine and exacerbate the situation don't affect it, keep in mind the possibility of a non-spinal related cause of your back pain.

This chapter and Chapter 3 are important for your understanding of the questions and choices you'll be confronted with as you consider the diagnosis and treatment of your back pain. In Chapter 5 we'll consider what you can and can't expect from diagnosis. Although diagnosing back pain is not always as definitive as you might like, the diagnostic process is essential to designing a treatment plan that will work for you.

Chapter : 5

Getting a Diagnosis

The complex workings of your back and the potential for a malfunction of one or more of its parts for any one of a number of reasons are what make identifying the source of back pain so difficult. One of the most challenging aspects of treating back pain is that we back doctors can never be too confident that we know the tissue responsible for a particular case of back pain. So when we say a person has a "sprain" or "strain," or a "painful disk," for that matter, we often can't be sure we're correct; and even the fanciest imaging test can't tell us. The good news here is that we often don't need to know the exact tissue that's awry in order to prescribe an effective treatment plan. That's the beauty of much of the back-pain research of the last several years: it permits us to make treatment decisions based upon the type and location of symptoms, without necessarily knowing the exact tissue of origin.

That said, most cases of low-back pain are garden-variety problems with pain centered in the low back with no features of nerve compression. We therefore typically assume these are due to sprains or strains. On the other hand, if the type and location of symptoms suggest another source of pain, for example, pain relating to a pinched nerve syndrome or an osteoporotic fracture, tests can be done to pinpoint the problem. This means the initial focus of diagnosis is to confirm which type of back disorder you have. Once we're sure of the type, we can assess whether further diagnostic tests might be helpful.

Diagnosis is a process of elimination. It's as important to rule out possible causes of back pain as it is to identify the actual cause. This takes time and may be frustrating for the back-pain sufferer. The experience of Theresa, my diagnostically discouraged patient in Chapter 1, who'd already done the rounds of a number of doctors' offices before she came to me, isn't that unusual. Sometimes a major frustration of back-pain sufferers isn't that they can't get a diagnosis, but that they get several conflicting ones, including being told there's nothing wrong! Theresa, though, had the correct approach. She was in pain. And people don't imagine back pain. She didn't give up seeking an answer as to why she was in pain. Neither should you. If your back is hurting, there's a reason. Like Theresa, think of diagnosis not so much as an answer, but as a search for an answer. An effective search involves logically moving through the diagnostic process one step at a time. Be patient; be persistent; become informed. Above all, keep in mind that although a successful search will guide you to the appropriate treatment options for your condition, it won't necessarily tell you everything you want to know, namely the precise source of your pain.

How Should I Begin My Search?

Your first step is to do nothing. Most backs will heal themselves without the need of medical intervention. The exceptions to letting nature take its course are if you suspect an emergency situation such as a cauda equina syndrome or an infection in the spine; if your back pain is intensifying over several days; or if your back pain is intense enough to prevent you from doing ordinary daily tasks and has lasted from seven to ten days. The first scenario—symptoms suggesting cauda equina syndrome, infection, and other emergencies—requires immediate action. The latter two, although not emergency situations, suggest that something other than garden-variety sprain or strain of the soft tissues is going on and you should find out what is wrong.

When Should I Call My Doctor?

Call your doctor *immediately* if you have the following symptoms along with your back pain

- Any bowel or bladder control problems
- Numbness in your groin or anal area
- Weakness in your legs
- Fever and chills with new back pain

Call your doctor *within a week* if your back pain

- Is intense enough to prevent you from doing your ordinary daily activities
- Has lasted for more than seven to ten days
- Doesn't seem to be improving

No need to call your doctor if

- Your back pain has lasted for less than seven to ten days
- It's noticeably improving each day
- You don't have any of the emergency symptoms listed above

Visit a Doctor, But Which One?

Diagnosing back pain is an intriguing marriage of art and science in which today's high-tech diagnostic tools initially play a less predominant role than the physician's age-old art of asking questions, listening to the patient's answers, and conducting a physical examination. So begin your search with a visit to your regular doctor. Back pain is a common problem and it is likely that your doctor sees a fair bit of it and will be able to help you.

In this era of medical specialization, it's tempting to think that when you have backache the most sensible way to get an accurate and timely diagnosis is to go to a doctor who specializes in back disorders. Well, probably not—at least not in the early days of your back problem. Rather than making an appointment to see a specialist, start with your primary care doctor—a competent medical generalist.

There are a number of reasons why your doctor should be your first stop. First, your primary care doctor knows you and has your medical records. He or she is therefore familiar with your overall state of health, including any conditions that increase your risk for certain types of back problems. Your doctor also presumably knows something about your lifestyle, including knowing if the risk factors for back disease discussed in Chapter 2 apply to you. All this information adds pieces to the diagnostic jigsaw puzzle, which also includes your detailed description of your symptoms and your doctor conducting a physical examination. Second, while you may need to visit a specialist at some point during the diagnostic process, the question of which specialist is appropriate for your situation is not usually apparent right away. A variety of medical specialists treat back pain, including orthopedic surgeons, neurosurgeons, neurologists, physiatrists, and rheumatologists. Although very knowledgeable about their specialties, specialists generally look first for conditions they are most familiar with. For example, a neurologist may be more likely to look and test for nerve pain as the cause of your backache. So first make an appointment with your primary care physician, who after evaluating you will discuss what, if anything, to do next, including who next to see if that's appropriate.

A Well-Prepared Medical History

Even if you have visited your primary care doctor regularly for checkups, don't expect him or her to remember everything about you, despite having access to your medical records. It's your job to bring your doctor up-to-date by being as informative as possible, which is why your doctor will prompt you through your medical history before physically examining you.

I can't emphasize enough how important it is for you to give your doctor the fullest medical history you can. Just as you would prepare for any important discussion, I strongly recommend that you prepare your medical history ahead of time, including writing it down. Your carefully prepared account will not only help point you and your doctor in the right direction, it will also minimize the risk of either one of you jumping to wrong conclusions and going off on a diagnostic wild goose chase. Calling your medical history an account is a little misleading; it is more of a dialogue, with your doctor asking you questions and you supplying as much detail as you can about your current situation and any past illnesses and injuries. Be prepared to answer questions such as:

* Did your back pain come on suddenly or gradually over time?
* Did anything happen that might have brought it on? For instance, did the pain start with an injury, such as an athletic or car injury, a fall, or a blow to your back or head? Or did you

notice pain after a specific activity, such as lifting something heavy, a long drive, or a new pillow (for neck pain)?

- Where in your back do you feel the pain? Describe the location as precisely as possible. Do you have pain elsewhere, such as in your buttocks, legs, and feet; thighs and hips; shoulders; arms; or chest?

- Can you describe your pain? Does it ache, stab, shoot, or burn? Do you feel it constantly, or does it come and go? Have you had similar pain in other parts of your back?

- Do you have other sensations along with the pain? Do you feel numbness, tingling ("pins and needles"), weakness, or stiffness anywhere in your back, legs, arms, or in other areas of your body?

- Is your pain worse or better at particular times of the day? Does it wake you up at night? Is it worse in the morning when you first get up?

- Does your pain get worse as the day progresses?

- What makes your pain worse? Do certain positions seem to aggravate your pain whereas others alleviate it? Are you more comfortable sitting, standing, walking, or lying down?

- Does moving about aggravate or alleviate your pain? What activities intensify or relieve your pain?

- Is this the first episode of back pain you've had? Have you previously had back surgery? If so, what was it for?

- What treatments have you had for your back pain so far, if any? Prescription and over-the-counter medications? Physical therapy? Injections? Alternative therapies? Write your previous treatments in a list and include dosages. Also be sure to note whether you found the treatment helpful.

- Do any close members of your family have arthritis or other diseases that might affect the spine?

- How are you feeling otherwise? Do you have other symptoms of illness, such as fever, weight loss, anemia, dizziness, nausea, blurry vision, difficulty concentrating, or depression?
- Do you have other chronic illnesses, such as osteo- or rheumatoid arthritis, diabetes, heart disease, or pelvic or abdominal conditions? What treatment are you receiving for these illnesses?
- Do you have a history of cancer? Have you had radiation treatment? Chemotherapy? Are you taking immunosuppressive medication?

Because they are risk factors, your doctor will no doubt ask you about your work, sports activities, hobbies, and possible sources of physical and emotional stress in your life at the present time.

The Value of the Physical Examination

After taking your medical history, your doctor will perform a general physical exam that will probably start with watching you stand, sit, and walk. He or she will assess your range of motion by asking you to bend forward, backward, and to the sides. Your doctor will also lift your legs and move your arms, shoulders, and neck. He or she will test your reflexes, especially those of the knee and ankle for low-back-pain sufferers and biceps and triceps for neck-pain sufferers; assess your muscle strength, particularly the strength of the muscles in your legs and feet for low-back-pain sufferers; and shoulders, arms, and wrists for neck pain sufferers. Your doctor will look for areas of tenderness by pressing on various muscles; and check the sensation in your legs, feet, arms, and hands. If any of these maneuvers are uncomfortable or painful, you should speak up. This is not the time to be stoically silent. Your input is essential, helping your doctor close in on the possible source of your pain.

To search for signs of irritated nerve roots, which are typically due to herniated lumbar disks, your doctor will administer the straight-leg-raising test. This test, which pulls on the sciatic nerve, can produce pain in your leg if the nerve root is irritated as happens when a disk is pressing on it. If individual reflexes and muscles are affected and your doctor can establish the precise location of any numbness or tingling, it's often possible to identify which nerve root or roots are affected. Similarly, in the cervical spine it's possible to discern which nerve is being compressed by a herniated disk or bone spur by checking your response to a gentle pinprick or light brush with a cotton swab at various points on your arms and hands. A careful history and physical examination are generally all that is needed to make a reasonably secure diagnosis. Imaging studies can confirm the diagnosis pathoanatomically and may provide a road map for interventions.

When Imaging Tests Are Helpful

It's tempting to want to enlist technology from the get-go in the hope that the indisputable power of imaging studies will be able to circumvent the more plodding approaches to diagnosing the cause of your back pain. But there are reasons why immediately turning to imaging techniques isn't an advantage and is often a disadvantage. This is particularly the case for sprain-and-strain injuries, the most common type of back pain. I'm not alone in this opinion. Most experts now question the value of early imaging tests for garden-variety, acute, nonspecific low-back pain. The current consensus among back doctors is that diagnostic imaging tends to be overused at the onset of back-pain symptoms—the very time when it is most unnecessary and less effective.

Why are x-rays and other more sophisticated imaging tests, such as computed tomography (CT) and magnetic resonance imaging (MRI), not initially useful in determining the cause of low-back pain in most cases? One reason is the technology itself. What type of tissue is it designed to illuminate? Does your back problem reside in that tissue? At the start of an episode of back pain you may not know the answer to that question. A second reason is the results of these types of imaging tests are often abnormal, yet the abnormalities they reveal are seldom related to the symptoms of your back pain. Consider that MRI shows disk herniations in one out of every five people who have *no back pain whatsoever*. A third reason, and probably the most convincing of all, is that about 90 percent of people with low-back pain recover on their own without such tests, often in a matter of weeks. In fact, one randomized controlled trial showed that there was no advantage to ordering an MRI early in the course of back pain. Outcomes were similar if the tests were ordered later as necessary or simply not ordered at all. There's also a cost consideration. CTs and MRIs are expensive tests, a factor for individuals, insurance companies, or governments to consider, depending upon whether you contribute to your health insurance coverage or if you live in a country where there is a single-payer system. Whatever the system, the tab for these costly tests must be paid.

However, there are times when imaging tests are very appropriate. For instance, if an initial medical evaluation leads your doctor to suspect a serious condition such as a tumor, infection, fracture, or compression of the cauda equina; or if the pain becomes chronic (continues with little or no improvement for three months or more), imaging studies and other tests may help identify the source of your back pain. And if you are considering having back

When Early Imaging Pays Off

In some circumstances it makes sense to use sophisticated imaging techniques early in the diagnostic process. I first met Ellen when she was in her midfifties. At that time, Ellen, generally a very active woman, was essentially housebound because of excruciating pain. Based on Ellen's description of her symptoms—tingling, numbness, and burning sensations—I felt confident that Ellen was suffering from compression of a sciatic nerve. Rather than waiting, Ellen wanted something done quickly to relieve her intense sciatica. I thought she would benefit from an epidural steroid injection, so I immediately sent her for an MRI to provide the physician who would do the injection with precise information about where to insert the needle. Ellen's MRI showed the exact location of her problem—a disk protrusion between L-4 and L-5, which was putting pressure on the L-5 nerve root. Ellen had an epidural injection, which brought her relief and got her mobile again. This window of pain relief meant that Ellen and I could work on a more permanent exercise-based treatment plan.

surgery, sophisticated imaging tests are essential to identify the exact location of your problem.

Let me summarize the place of CTs and MRIs in the diagnosis of back pain. Unless your doctor suspects a severe or systemic condition that needs immediate attention, it's best to adopt a wait-and-watch strategy for at least four weeks before considering the more sophisticated imaging tests. Chances are you'll recover on your own. But if you don't, and if you and your doctor agree an imaging test would be helpful, here's what to expect.

X-Ray: The Workhorse of Imaging Technologies

Plain x-rays (see Figure 5.1), also known as *radiographs*, primarily show your bones and the spaces between them, as well as other calcium-containing tissues by projecting a picture onto a piece of film. (Some of the newer x-rays use electronic imaging techniques rather than film to achieve the same result.) While giving some idea of the condition of the vertebrae, x-rays of the spine provide little information about the disks, muscles, ligaments, and other soft tissues. One concern about x-rays, which has been voiced over the years, is exposure to radiation. X-rays do expose you to some radiation, but the doses are low and in the absence of other, significant radiation exposure, shouldn't pose a danger.

A major drawback of x-rays is that an astounding 90 percent of x-rays in people over age fifty show spinal abnormalities resulting from degenerative changes due to aging. The conundrum is that such age-related changes are also visible in the x-rays of individuals who do not have back pain, meaning you can't assume such abnormalities are the cause of your problem. In other words, the wear and tear of aging you see on your x-ray may not be the source of your pain. This drawback is not limited to x-rays. A high percentage of abnormalities are seen in the more sophisticated types of imaging, too. As we discussed earlier, one in five asymptomatic persons has a disk herniation on MRI and about one in five has lumbar spinal stenosis. Among persons over sixty years old, 90 percent have disk bulges, making these findings essentially normal features of aging.

Nonetheless, despite their limited diagnostic value in some situations, x-rays are indispensable for identifying bone fractures, as well as bone changes caused by tumors, infection, and certain forms of arthritis.

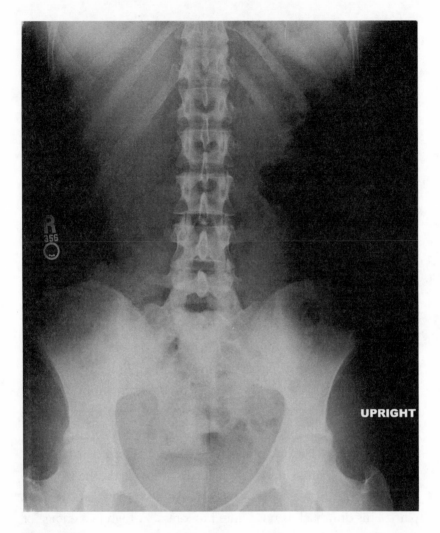

Figure 5.1

X-Ray of the Spine

An x-ray, or radiograph, primarily shows bones and other tissues that contain calcium.

Computed Tomography (CT) Scans

Computed tomography (CT)—also referred to as *computerized axial tomography* (CAT)—utilizes a more sophisticated x-ray machine that gathers multiple images and a computer program that turns these images into cross-sectional images of tissues and organs (see Figure 5.2).

For a CT scan, you lie still on a table that slides into a tunnel-like scanner. The x-ray tube moves along your body taking multiple pictures, each from a slightly different angle. Instead of sending a single x-ray beam through your body, this device uses many narrow

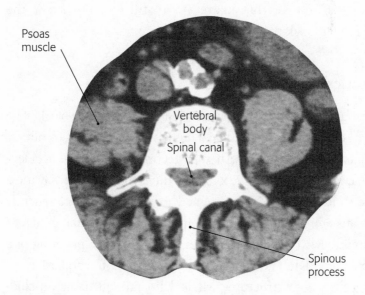

Figure 5.2

CT Scan

Computed tomography, also known as a "CT scan," provides cross-sectional images of the body and shows distinct outlines of the various structures.

COURTESY OF DR. DANIEL ROSENTHAL, MASSACHUSETTS GENERAL HOSPITAL.

beams. The beams are collected by a detector that rotates around you and are sent to the specialized computer, which instantaneously analyzes and synthesizes multiple images of your back. The result is a set of remarkably detailed composite views in almost any anatomic plane. A CT scan takes about twenty minutes. A downside is that CT scans expose you to much more radiation than regular x-rays.

CT scans have become ubiquitous in modern medicine because they can visualize several different types of tissue, including bone, soft tissue, and blood vessels. But despite their amazing versatility, CT scans aren't a panacea when it comes to diagnosing back disorders. Consequently, even after having a CT scan (or any other sophisticated test for that matter), you still may not know the source of your back pain.

Magnetic Resonance Imaging (MRI)

MRI technology is the relatively new kid on the imaging block. The first MRI exam was performed on a human in 1977 (and took almost five hours!). Contrast this with x-ray technology that was accidentally invented in 1895. Unlike x-ray machines that are relatively inexpensive, MRI machines are extremely expensive and consequently MRI scans are very costly. Costs vary from one hospital, clinic, or freestanding MRI facility to another, but expect the price tag of a lumbar spine MRI to range from one to two thousand dollars.

As well as bony structures, MRIs delineate soft tissues, including intervertebral disks, spinal nerves, and tumors (see Figure 5.3). The technology uses electromagnetic waves to create images of your tissues, thus avoiding the radiation hazard of x-rays and CT scans. Detailed images are obtained from the minute electromagnetic waves emitted by body tissues that are subjected to an intense magnetic field.

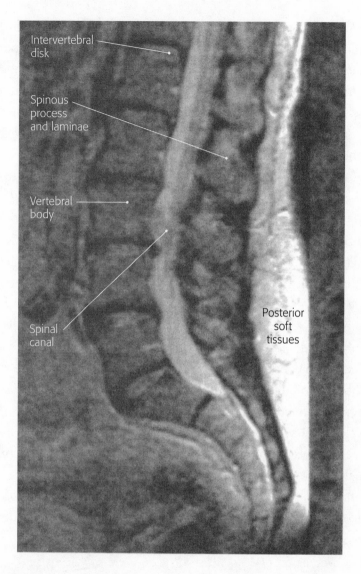

Figure 5.3

Magnetic Resonance Imaging

Like a CT scan, magnetic resonance imaging, also known as an "MRI," provides images of your body in different planes, as well as showing soft tissues in considerable detail.

COURTESY OF DR. DANIEL ROSENTHAL, MASSACHUSETTS GENERAL HOSPITAL.

An MRI scan usually takes half an hour or longer, during which you must lie motionless in a large tube—a giant magnet—situated in the center of a very large and loud machine. Although MRI is so noisy that you may wish to wear soundproof ear protectors, the procedure is not invasive in any way and is believed to be completely harmless. However, some people feel claustrophobic in the tube or find it difficult to stay still for the time required. Institutions usually offer a choice of music for you to listen to on stereo headphones as a way of distracting you from the noise and your circumstances. Some institutions suggest you bring your own choice of music from home. I've offered patients mild antianxiety medication to take just before having an MRI. This is often helpful for patients who feel anxious in the scanner.

MRIs produce very detailed and clear images. The downside of the test, as I've previously mentioned, is that when the test reveals an abnormality, it isn't necessarily the source of your back pain. Indeed, it may not cause any pain at all. MRI scans of adults with *no* back pain have revealed disk bulges or protrusions in the lumbar spine in nearly two-thirds of cases. Another limitation is that people who have implanted electromagnetic devices such as pacemakers or aneurysm clips can't be scanned by an MRI machine. You'll also be asked if you have any orthopedic screws, plates, and joints. These are typically not electromagnetic and therefore don't rule out an MRI, but because they distort the image, the reader of the scan needs to know about them.

Myelography

In this test, a contrast medium (a fluid opaque to x-rays) is injected into the spinal canal and its flow is observed with a fluoroscope, a special x-ray machine. The resultant x-ray, called a *myelogram*, allows a doctor to locate any abnormalities—such as herniated disks, stenosis, or spinal tumors—that cause distortion of the spinal canal or exiting nerve sheaths. Myelography can reveal the positions of the lumbar nerve roots as they course through and exit the spinal canal. It can also indicate distortions in the shape of the spinal cord and the cauda equina. The test will also show fractures, dislocations, osteoporosis, and deformities in the curve of the spine. Myelography is often combined with CT scanning (producing a CT myelogram). This is a powerful technology capable of detecting many abnormalities.

Myelography is expensive. It must be performed in a hospital radiology department or in a clinic by an x-ray technician. It is also invasive in that it requires injecting fluid into your spinal cord. And some people find it quite uncomfortable. Possible complications include headache (which can occasionally be severe), allergic reaction to the contrast fluid, and even infection resulting from the injection of the fluid, although this is rare. Since the advent of newer imaging techniques, myelography is performed only when a diagnosis is particularly difficult; or when a doctor and patient have decided that surgery is needed and the problem area must be precisely located. In such situations, the spinal surgeon will typically order a CT myelogram.

Other Diagnostic Procedures

Upon occasion, a doctor will recommend other tests. As with the imaging tests already described, these are useful once your doctor has ruled out some probable causes of your pain and is therefore using these tests to further narrow the possibilities.

Bone Scan

A bone scan is used to diagnose tumor, infection, or certain fractures. When a virtually harmless, short-lived radioactive substance absorbed by bone is injected into a person's bloodstream, the amount soaked up varies according to the activity of the bone cells. Absorption of the material can be recorded on photographic film by an electronic device, thereby locating areas of rapid bone formation. A tumor, an infection, or a healing fracture will appear as a hot spot on the film. Once the location of an abnormality is known, other techniques can be used to make the diagnosis. A bone scan, which is nearly as expensive as CT, takes about four hours from the time of the injection of the radioactive material to completion of the study. The exposure to radioactivity associated with this procedure is less than 10 percent of that required for three regular x-rays of the spine. The only discomfort is having the injection and lying facedown for up to an hour while the scan is completed.

Electromyography (EMG) and Nerve Conduction Testing

Electromyography assesses the electrical activity of your muscles. Nerve conduction testing assesses the peripheral nerves. Together, these procedures provide a great deal of information about the function of peripheral nerves, nerve roots, and the muscles that these nerves supply. In patients with spinal disorders, these tests are very helpful in establishing a diagnosis. Both procedures may be uncomfortable, with EMG typically being more uncomfortable than nerve conduction testing. In electromyography, fine needles are inserted into your muscles to detect and record their electrical patterns, either in response to electrical stimulation of nerves or through voluntary muscle activity. You may be asked to move a little during the test. For nerve conduction testing, small electrodes are place on your skin through which you'll get a mild shock. The test provides the examiner with data on the amount of time it takes for the nerve impulse to travel from one electrode to another.

Blood Tests

Your doctor won't routinely use blood tests to diagnose the cause of your back problem, but they can be useful in some instances.

- A complete blood count (CBC), which includes counts of the red cells and white cells, can highlight a problem such as an infection or inflammation.
- The erythrocyte sedimentation rate, or "sed" rate, is a measure of inflammation that may suggest infection, some forms of arthritis, or a tumor.
- The C-reactive protein (CRP) test is a more recent addition to testing. It's used as a nonspecific marker of inflammation.

Daunting though the diagnostic process may seem, a measured approach will give you the information you need to embark on the treatment decision process. In the long run, your time and patience at this stage will be rewarded by finding the right treatment for your back pain. Naturally, whatever diagnosis you receive, your uppermost concern is pain relief. In Chapter 6, I'll discuss the various traditional approaches to pain control for your hurting back.

Part III

Controlling Your Pain

Chapter : 6

Priority Number One: Relieving Your Pain

The first five chapters of this book have provided you with what you need to make informed decisions about managing your back pain. From here on we'll be looking at the forms that management of your problem can take. First and foremost is the management of pain. Although in subsequent chapters we'll be looking at the pros and cons of nonsurgical treatments, the pivotal role of exercise in rehabilitation and preventing recurrences, and surgical treatments, the first step in any back-pain management program is to reign in the pain you're experiencing. Pain control is a number one priority.

Simply put, your back hurts. You can't turn, bend, or perhaps sleep through the night without experiencing a considerable degree of discomfort. No wonder you feel miserable. Why you hurt may understandably be less important to you than putting an end to your discomfort. At the start of an episode of back pain, all anyone wants is for the pain to go away and life to get back to normal.

For most cases of sprain-and-strain backache, that's precisely what will happen. Your pain will ease with the passage of time and the help of a home remedy or an over-the-counter medication. In a matter of days or weeks, you'll be back in your old routine. But this isn't true for everyone, and it often isn't true for some of the other types of back problems. Let me qualify that last remark: some people experience longer-lasting pain and seek medical help. But whether the pain lasts a short or longer time, pain is the number one symptom of most back problems and pain relief is the first milestone on any road to recovery. Back-pain sufferers aren't alone in this. Relieving pain is a fundamental human instinct and seeking pain relief is the single most common reason that people see the doctor. That's certainly true in my practice: most patients visit me for the first time seeking relief from pain.

What Is Pain?

Pain is like a pirate who comes from nowhere and takes over your life. We tend to think of pain as a physical sensation only, but it can be more than that. Back pain, when it persists, can depress you emotionally, interfere with your ability to work, and prevent you from enjoying the company of your family and friends.

In the medical setting, *pain* is a term that describes a neuronal signaling system. This system relays messages between the part of the body that encounters a noxious stimulus and the brain, where pain is "perceived." Indeed, if the brain doesn't "perceive" the message as a pain report and respond to it as such, you won't feel pain. This signaling system can be switched on by anything the body perceives as "dangerous," such as a burn, trauma, surgery, cancer, or, in terms of this book, disorders of the back. After reporting the problem to the brain, the relay system conveys the brain's instruction that you get away from or not enter into the danger zone where the point of pain is located. In terms of back pain, this translates into avoiding making movements that will tax the specific areas of the back where you hurt. Looked at this way, pain is a protection and not a problem.

Back pain, as I noted earlier, can run the gamut from a passing inconvenience to a debilitating chronic condition, meaning that for some people relieving their pain is the only treatment required; whereas for others, alleviating their pain is but one part of a multi-part treatment plan. How much pain, and how long an individual is willing to tolerate it, influences that person's treatment decisions, especially the decision of whether to adopt a wait-and-see approach or to consider surgical options sooner rather than later. In this chapter I'll be giving you an overview of how pain works—the pain pathways—followed by the particulars of various pain relief treatments used in the treatment of back pain.

Pain: Out with the Old; In with the New

In some ancient cultures pain was considered a punishment sent by the gods for evil doings. Not so very many years ago pain was something patients had to endure because of the limited pain relief options available. Fortunately, times have changed. In recent years, huge strides have been made in understanding pain, in particular:

- Pain has a neurobiological basis that can be studied, leading to better pain control treatments.

- The study of pain has become a medical specialty in its own right. This has given rise to doctors who specialize in the treatment of pain and to multidisciplinary pain clinics for patients who suffer from long-term debilitating pain.

- The medical profession as a whole has become more aware of the need to treat pain and better informed as to how best to do that. In fact, pain is sometimes referred to as the "fifth" vital sign—along with the four traditional vitals of temperature, pulse, blood pressure, and rate of respirations—underscoring its importance.

- Significant advances have been made in the development of new medications and non-drug therapies. Researchers now know what kind of nerve cells send pain signals to the spinal cord and brain and where in the brain those signals are received. This has led to an understanding of how certain drugs work to ease pain.

But the treatment of pain is an emerging field, and many questions remain unanswered. Moreover, pain differs from person to person. Family upbringing, cultural influences, attitude, and past pain experiences interact to shape an individual's perception of pain. Although there's a wealth of knowledge about how the mechanics of pain work in the brain, the nuances of a person's subjective response are still largely unpredictable. What is tolerable for one person may be close to unbearable for another. Given this complexity, researchers are unlikely to stumble on a magic on/off switch for pain anytime soon—if ever. Instead, back-pain management strives toward the more attainable goal of *minimizing physical discomfort while maximizing your ability to function*. This is doable because today you and your doctor can draw upon an ever-broadening array of pain treatments. However, because people respond differently to pain and what works well for one person may work less well for someone else, you should be prepared to be flexible. For the treatment of chronic back pain especially, you may have to combine several different therapies to create a treatment plan that offers you relief. Ultimately, the best treatment for your back pain is the treatment that works best for you. That may sound circular but it's true. You'll need to try a few things and determine which works best for you.

Can You Define Pain?

Everyone knows what pain is, but defining pain in words isn't so easy. The word "pain" comes from the Latin word "poena," meaning penalty or punishment, and unfortunately pain still carries that negative, moral-laced connotation. Medical definitions tend to use words like "discomfort" or "distress" that essentially just say "pain" in some other way. Pain researchers often use the definition developed by the International Association for the Study of Pain that describes pain as "an unpleasant sensory or emotional experience associated with actual or potential tissue damage, or described in terms of such damage."

Most pain specialists think of pain as having four components: detection of damage to human tissue; the brain's perception of that damage; the emotional response to that perception; and the behaviors in response to those emotions and perceptions.

For people whose backs are hurting, the only definition that really matters is that they hurt. Or as two prominent pain researchers wrote several years ago: pain is "whatever the experiencing person says it is, existing whenever he [or she] says it does."

Classifying Your Pain by Its Duration

Back pain is classified according to what causes it and how long it lasts. I discussed the causes of back pain in Chapter 4; now I'll talk about your back pain based on its duration. Using this yardstick, there are three basic types of back pain: acute, subacute, and chronic.

Acute and Subacute Pain

Acute and subacute back pain can come on abruptly or come on gradually, steadily increasing in intensity. Although it can be severe, ultimately the pain associated with both acute and subacute back pain is finite. Back doctors categorize acute pain as pain that lasts up to a month and subacute as lasting anywhere from one month to six months. But the boundary between subacute pain and long-lasting or chronic pain is sometimes blurry. Any pain that continues for more than a few months causes physical and emotional changes that muddy the distinction between subacute and chronic. Moreover, even brief periods of pain are capable of causing the kind of long-term changes to nerve cells that can permanently excite them and lead to chronic pain.

Chronic Pain

This type of pain can start with an injury or disease but persists well after the injury is healed or the disease is cured. Some pain experts prefer the term "persistent pain." One prominent pain researcher wrote that with chronic pain, "It is almost as if the brain develops a memory for pain, much like the skill of learning to ride a bicycle is never unlearned." A variety of conditions—such as cancer, arthritis, diabetic neuropathy, and back pain—are recognized sources of chronic pain.

How Pain Works

The simple answer, as I touched on earlier, is that pain is a relay signal that starts in nerve cells where the point of pain is located and travels via nerves in that location to the spinal cord and on to the brain where the pain is "perceived." Let me expand on this. Once it reaches the brain, the signal makes its way to various regions of the brain, some of which control thinking and emotion and others that control reactions to pain (see Figure 6.1). You respond to the brain's perception of pain by avoiding what stimulates the pain signal, for example, by not completing a forward bend to pick up a pen you dropped on the floor.

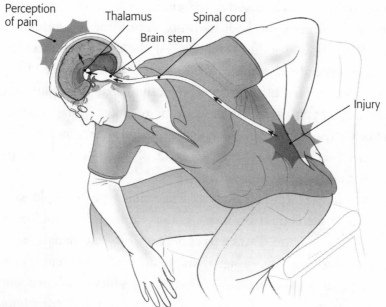

Figure 6.1

The Perception of Pain

When you have pain in your back, the signal travels via nerves to and up the spinal cord and into a part of the brain called the *thalamus*. The thalamus sends the signal to several parts of the brain, including those that control touch, emotion, physical reaction, and memory.

At this level, pain is no different from any other sensory experience: there's a stimulus, a message gets sent through the nervous system, and the spinal cord and brain react to that message. Maybe this is all you want to know. However, to understand how various types of pain treatments control pain, which is especially important if you suffer from chronic back pain, you need to look more closely at the workings of the nervous system.

Nerves and Receptors of the Nervous System

Nerve cells, called *neurons,* are the frontline of the nervous system. Neurons come in several shapes and sizes. Most neurons resemble spiders, with a small central body and several long, leglike protrusions. Neurons bundle together to form nerve fibers or nerves that extend throughout the body. Sensory nerves carry information from the outside world to the brain. At the ends of these nerve fibers are specialized sensors, called *nociceptors* (pronounced NO-seh-SEP-ters). They play a key role in receiving painful stimuli and transmitting pain signals by responding to injury, inflammation, and other tissue changes. When magnified, nociceptors look like the frayed end of a rope. Not every organ of the body has nociceptors, but muscles and joints do.

Once a nociceptor is activated by some type of unpleasant stimulus, it sends the pain message along a nerve in the form of an electrical impulse. Two kinds of nerves carry pain signals. Each carries a different type of signal and relays it at a different speed. One type carries the first sharp pain and transmits signals at about forty miles per hour. The other type carries the dull, throbbing pain that follows, sending these signals along at only about three miles per hour.

When the signal reaches the nerve ending, specialized chemicals known as *neurotransmitters* are called into action. Different types of neurotransmitters are involved in the transmission of pain signals. Certain neurotransmitters dampen or block a pain signal from being sent on, while others convey the pain signal to neighboring nerve cells (see Figure 6.2). The pain impulse is transmitted in this manner along peripheral nerves and into the spinal cord.

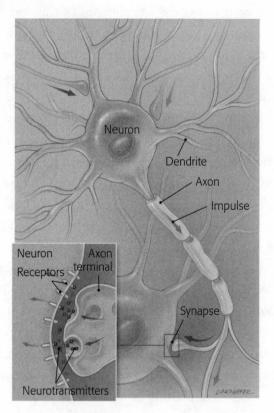

Figure 6.2

Pain Signals on the Go

A pain message travels through the body from one nerve cell (neuron) to the next. The signal passes down the axon of one neuron and travels across a small gap called a *synapse* to reach the next neuron. To transmit signals, the neuron releases chemical messengers called *neurotransmitters* into the synapse between it and the next neuron. The neurotransmitters attach to receptors on neighboring neurons and allow the message to continue on its way. This process is repeated in rapid succession between nerve cells throughout the body, up the spinal cord, and into the brain.

The transfer point of pain signals from the peripheral nerves to the spinal cord is a dense array of nerve cells known collectively as the *dorsal horn*. This network of nerves and nerve connections where incoming messages can be accentuated, dampened, or blocked altogether is the "sifting and sorting" office of the spinal cord. Once through the switchboard of the dorsal horn, the pain signals journey to the thalamus region of the brain, which dispatches them to other regions of the brain. Some signals reach the part of the brain responsible for spatial awareness, while others arrive in the limbic system, where emotions arise. Still others travel to the hypothalamus, which controls hormonal responses and such functions as sleep, body temperature, and appetite. Because the brain simultaneously processes pain information in so many disparate regions, human beings have an understandably complex and multilayered response to painful stimuli.

Sometimes this signaling system goes awry. For example, the cells of the dorsal horn can become overly stimulated—which can heighten pain or increase its frequency. If nerves continually barrage the dorsal horn with pain signals, the nerve cells there can become more sensitive and excitable. When a weak signal, or one that would not ordinarily be a pain signal at all, comes in, the now hypersensitive dorsal horn nerve cells overreact. What would normally be experienced as mild pain is instead experienced as severe pain. An analogy is a sensor light on the back of your house. If the sensor is set too sensitively, every small, snuffling nocturnal creature will trigger the switch and flood your yard with light like a night game at a stadium. You can easily reset your backyard sensor light; it's not so easy to "reset" your body's response to pain signals.

Three Principles of Pain Relief

Just as the forward motion of a row of tumbling dominos can be interrupted by removing one tile, pain signals can be thwarted by disrupting the elaborate electrochemical communication system between nerve cells. This interruption is the foundation for nearly all pain treatment approaches. The three principal ways of relieving pain can be boiled down to the following:

- Blocking the ability of a nerve to carry pain signals by interfering with the electrical impulses traveling through the nerve
- Blocking the action of the neurotransmitters that relay pain signals between nerves
- Enhancing the action of systems in the body that inhibit pain signals from being passed on

Your Body's Natural Pain Relief Plan

Long before humans evolved to the point of seeking remedies for pain, the body devised internal systems to temper the onslaught of unpleasant sensations. These natural systems have guided scientists and doctors in developing new ways of managing pain.

Endorphins: Chemical Scouts

Over time, scientists have come to understand that pain is naturally modulated by the release of pain-suppressing proteins by the brain and the pituitary gland, a pea-sized gland at the base of the brain. These pain suppressors include enkephalin and larger proteins called *endorphins*. Scientists began looking for these natural chemicals after discovering that the painkilling drug morphine attaches to specific receptors on brain and spinal cord cells. It made sense that the body would also produce substances that fit those receptors or why else would they be there? As a result of this research, endorphins were first identified in 1975. Endorphins help offset pain signals traveling up to the brain, in effect reducing the sensation of pain. Some current pain relief techniques—such as transcutaneous electrical nerve stimulation (TENS), relaxation, some complementary therapies, and exercise—work in part by inducing the release of endorphins.

Neurotransmitters: Neuronal Border Guards

Other natural chemicals can help filter out pain signals. For instance, while neurotransmitters play a key role in conveying signals between neurons, not all neurotransmitters pass pain signals along. Some of these chemicals are what's called "inhibitory" and block pain signals from being sent. Examples include the neurotransmitters serotonin and norepinephrine, which can dampen pain signals. This understanding has led to the treatment of pain with medications that boost levels of serotonin and norepinephrine, such as certain antidepressant medications.

The Gate Control Theory of Pain

You may be somewhat familiar with endorphins and neurotransmitters as part of the pain picture, but did you know about the influence of the gate control theory of pain control that paved the way for our understanding of them? The gate control theory, which was formulated in 1965, was instrumental in introducing the idea that pain had a biological basis that could be studied. This meant that rather than being something magical, which inexplicably came and went, pain could be subjected to scientific research that would yield measurable results.

The gate control theory works as follows: interneurons (small nerve cells that bridge the gap between larger neurons) in the spinal cord function as gatekeepers for pain signals. If the finer-diameter nerve fibers of the body (those relaying pain signals) are stimulated, they act on these interneurons and the gate opens. A pain signal is then sent on to the brain and you hurt. But if signals come from other, larger nerve fibers (those relaying touch and pressure signals), the interneurons garble the message and the gate doesn't open. What determines the gate opening and pain messages reaching the brain is the balance between these two sets of nerve fibers. An example is that rubbing your back where it hurts, which seems a strange thing to do, can actually make you feel better.

The gate control theory had a profound effect on pain medicine. For the first time, doctors began to design therapies that would combat pain by stimulating other kinds of nerves. As a result, they developed new forms of treatment such as transcutaneous electrical nerve stimulation (TENS) and spinal cord stimulation. The gate control theory also helped lend theoretical credibility to therapeutic massage and a host of other complementary treatments. A cautionary note: subsequent studies, however, question how effective TENS and some complementary treatments, which initially looked promising, are for back-pain relief.

Once More with Feeling: Describe Your Back Pain

Up until now, I've filled you in on how pain works overall in your body. To relieve your back pain, however, you need to match the type of pain you have with an appropriate pain relief medicine or therapy. What does your back pain feel like? Can you describe it? Is your back stiff? Does it ache? Do you feel a sharp pain or hear a grinding noise when you turn your head or body? Back pain isn't all the same. It can be mild or severe, achy or sharp, stationary or shooting. It may stand alone or be accompanied by other trouble-some complaints. Likewise pain medications aren't all the same. The better you can identify the type of pain you have, the faster you'll get your pain under control.

Name That Back Pain

Although descriptions of pain tend to be somewhat subjective, the following pointers should help you identify the pain type you have. These pointers will also help you describe your symptoms to your doctor.

• **Muscle pain.** An ache or soreness in the muscles that support the cervical and lumbar spine may occur in response to over-exertion, prolonged physical stress (usually from poor back positioning during everyday activities), emotional tension, or fibromyalgia. Muscles may also develop hard knots that are sore to the touch, sometimes called "trigger points." In fibro-myalgia, places that are painful when pressed are called "ten-der points."

• **Muscle spasm.** This is a sudden, powerful contraction of back muscles. When you wake up with a painful stiff neck, that's likely a muscle spasm—what is sometimes called a "crick" in your neck. The muscle usually feels painful, tight, or knotted, and may be impossible to move; or you may feel it "twitch-ing." Muscle spasms, which can happen in any of the muscles of the back, result from a muscle injury, but they may also occur if there is a deeper problem—say, in a disk or nerve. In those instances, the muscle tenses in order to stabilize the back and prevent you from moving in a way to cause pain or further damage. This is a reflex that you can't control volun-tarily and aren't even aware of until you notice the pain and feel the tense muscle. Neck muscle spasms sometimes accompany emotional stress.

- **Headache.** Neck-related headache, called *cervicogenic* headache or *cervical* headache, is most often felt in the back of the head and upper neck, where muscles extending along the skull are continuous with neck muscles that may become tense or go into spasm. Neck-related headache pain is typically dull or aching, rather than sharp. It is aggravated by neck movement and often accompanied by stiffness and tenderness of neck muscles. A headache, typically accompanied by fever, can also be a sign of an infection, including meningitis, which is quite serious. So when neck pain is accompanied by headache, it's important to note whether there is fever, rash, or any other signs of more serious illness and, if so, seek medical advice immediately.

- **Facet joint pain.** Often described as deep, sharp, or aching, facet joint pain typically worsens if you lean backward and toward the affected side and may radiate to other areas of your back or shoulders. Arthritis in the facet joints, as in other locations, may feel worse in the morning or after a period of inactivity.

- **Nerve pain.** Irritation or pinching of the roots of the spinal nerves causes pain that may be sharp, fleeting, often burning and frequently accompanied by pins and needles and numbness. Depending on the nerve involved, the pain may shoot down the leg or arm and be felt in the feet or hands.

- **Referred pain.** When you feel pain at a site removed from the area where the problem lies, it's called "referred" pain. A number of conditions, including pancreatitis and aortic aneurysm, may cause referred back pain. These are serious problems, but fortunately they are rare and have other clues that help determine the correct diagnosis.

- **Bone pain.** Pain and tenderness in the vertebrae is far less common than back pain from the soft tissues. Bone pain, a dull, deep, relentless pain sensation, is one of the worst types of pain and needs medical evaluation because it can stem from serious conditions such as cancer or infection as well as fracture.

Medicating Your Back Pain

Pain relief is the first step in the treatment of back pain. Whereas pain can protect against further injury, it isn't helpful in the healing process. You'll recover faster if your body's resources are available for healing rather than dealing with pain. And the relatively recent strides in pain research I discussed earlier in this chapter have led to the discovery of new pain medications or the refinement of existing medications that can be tailored to control even very severe back pain in most cases. The question no longer is can back pain be alleviated, but what would be the best medication with the least side effects for each individual case? You're familiar with the distinction between nonprescription or over-the-counter (OTC) and prescription medications. Medications that fall into the first category are typically less potent at the recommended dose than prescription medications. That doesn't mean, however, that all OTC medications come with an absolute guarantee of safety. You need to know what you are taking and how much is safe to take over what period of time.

Some medications are available as both prescription and non-prescription medications—albeit at different doses—such as ibuprofen and naproxen. Any product sold as a drug has undergone extensive clinical trials to prove it is safe and efficacious. In the United States, the Food and Drug Administration (FDA) is the government agency that licenses drugs for the U.S. market. Most countries have a drug classification system and licensing protocols that are determined by a government agency. (Drug-licensing protocols can vary from country to country.)

Over-the-Counter Pain Relievers

Virtually everyone has taken aspirin, ibuprofen (Advil, Motrin), naproxen sodium (Aleve), or acetaminophen (Tylenol) at one time or another (see Table 6.1). These over-the-counter—nonprescription—pain relievers are usually all that is needed to ease acute low-back pain. Aspirin, ibuprofen, and naproxen sodium are nonsteroidal anti-inflammatory drugs (NSAIDs) and as such have an advantage over acetaminophen in that they can reduce inflammation in strained tissues. They have the disadvantage that they also commonly cause gastric irritation and rarely gastrointestinal bleeding, as well as other problems, including asthma in some cases. But it's important to remember that any OTC medication can have toxic side effects, especially when taken in heavy doses over long periods of time.

What Are NSAIDs? Although they aren't steroids, NSAIDs, like steroids, dampen inflammation. Despite being a large class of drugs with many differences, all NSAIDs fundamentally work the same way: They block an enzyme called *cyclooxygenase* (COX) from converting arachidonic acid, a compound found in cell membranes, into several types of prostaglandins, molecules that play a key role in pain transmission and inflammation. Prostaglandin molecules function as town criers; they awaken the body's inflammatory response, causing swelling, pain, dilation of blood

Table 6.1

Common Over-the-Counter Medications

Drug Name	Brand Name	Time It Takes to Work	Duration
Acetaminophen	Tylenol	30 minutes	4–6 hours
Aspirin (acetylsalicylic acid)	Bayer, Bufferin, others	30 minutes	4–6 hours
Ibuprofen	Advil, Motrin, others	30 minutes	4–6 hours
Naproxen sodium	Aleve, Naprosyn	30 minutes	8–12 hours

vessels, and other phenomena. In concert with other molecules, prostaglandins also cause nerve cells to become more sensitive. By hampering the production of prostaglandins, NSAIDs ease or prevent pain. That's the good news. But prostaglandins also keep your stomach lining healthy, regulate blood flow to your kidneys, and enable platelets (components of blood) to initiate the blood-clotting process. Therefore, by interfering with the production of prostaglandins, NSAIDs can cause unwanted side effects such as ulcers, intestinal bleeding, hypertension, fluid retention, and impaired kidney function. NSAIDs are available as both prescription and nonprescription medications.

Acetaminophen, the active ingredient in Tylenol, is not an NSAID. It inhibits cyclooxygenase in the central nervous system

Maximum Daily Dose	Comments
4,000 mg	Not an NSAID. Fewer gastric side effects make it useful for mild pain. In high doses, possible liver and kidney toxicity. May be combined with opioids (Percocet, others) for more severe pain.
4,000 mg	Inhibits blood clotting for up to two weeks; shouldn't be used before or after surgery. Buffered and enteric-coated versions (Bufferin, Ecotrin) may be easier on your stomach. Drugs in the same salicylate group as aspirin—such as trisalicylate (Trilisate), diflunisal (Dolobid), and salsalate (Disalcid)—are preferred for people with stomach and bleeding problems.
2,400 mg	Safer and better tolerated than aspirin. Potent inhibitor of cyclooxygenase.
1,100 mg	Like ibuprofen, a derivative of propionic acid, and therefore has some of the same clinical characteristics. Stays in the blood longer than ibuprofen so it needs to be taken only twice a day. Higher rates of gastrointestinal side effects than ibuprofen.

but not elsewhere in the body. Unlike NSAIDs, acetaminophen does not cause ulcers or bleeding. Because this drug has few side effects in limited doses, many doctors recommend trying acetaminophen before using other OTC or prescription pain medications.

The COX-2 Inhibitor Controversy. COX-2 inhibitors are a class of NSAIDs. The cyclooxygenase enzyme has two forms: COX-1 and COX-2. COX-1 protects the stomach lining from stomach acids and it plays a role in kidney function; COX-2 is a by-product of joint injury and inflammation. The older, standard NSAIDs work by blocking both COX-1 and COX-2. Because of the unwelcome side effects that resulted from blocking the protective capability of COX-1, some years ago a new class of NSAIDs was developed to

Save Your Stomach, Harm Your Liver

People suffering from back pain sometimes choose a pain reliever that contains acetaminophen in order to avoid the stomach upset and gastrointestinal bleeding that can result from using aspirin or certain NSAIDs on a regular basis. But acetaminophen, like any drug, has its own risks—especially for the liver.

A 2005 study in the medical journal *Hepatology* concluded that acetaminophen was to blame for 42 percent of the cases of acute liver failure seen in American hospitals during a six-year study period. Although some of these cases were intentional suicide attempts, many of the poisonings were accidental.

To avoid an accidental poisoning, don't exceed the recommended maximum dose per day, which is generally set at 4 grams (4,000 milligrams), the equivalent of eight extra-strength Tylenol tablets. If you drink on a regular basis, it is wise to avoid acetaminophen altogether as the threshold for toxicity appears to be lower for those who drink than it is for other people.

block only COX-2. This group of prescription-only medications, which includes celecoxib (Celebrex), rofecoxib (Vioxx), and valdecoxib (Bextra), are no more potent than the standard NSAIDs. But they became bestsellers because they offered pain relief with less risk of the unwelcome gastrointestinal side effects that could accompany the long-term use of standard NSAIDs.

The COX-2 inhibitor bubble has recently burst. A link between COX-2 inhibitors and increased risk of cardiovascular problems—heart disease and stroke—has been confirmed. In light of the evidence, experts at the FDA and elsewhere are rethinking when and how these drugs should be used—and by whom. Here's the story so far. In 2004, the manufacturer of Vioxx voluntarily withdrew the drug from the marketplace, although it's possible it may return with a warning label. In the meantime, the manufacturer of Vioxx is engaged in extensive litigation with relatives of patients who died while taking the drug. In 2005, the manufacturer of Bextra also voluntarily withdrew its product from the marketplace. Celebrex is currently the only COX-2 inhibitor available in the United States. The FDA may take further regulatory action regarding Celebrex after analyzing the preliminary reports from one of several long-term studies conducted by the National Institutes of Health (NIH).

In 2005, the FDA contacted manufacturers of all NSAIDs—both prescription and OTC—requesting that they make labeling changes on their products to alert consumers to the possibility of increased risk of cardiovascular events.

Know What's in Your Medicine. Before we move on to a discussion of prescription medications, let me again emphasize that the nonprescription designation of a product is not a guarantee of the absolute safety of that product. As a precaution you should know what is in the medicine you are taking and what is considered a safe dose for that pharmacological agent. Of course, any information pertaining to the chemical composition of a licensed medicine must, by law, appear on the label. If you're not sure what you are taking, read the label and don't exceed the daily dose.

Prescription Pain Relievers

If your low-back pain is severe, as is often the case in nerve compression syndromes, or if your pain becomes chronic, your doctor may prescribe a stronger medication. This could be a stronger prescription dose of an OTC drug or another class of drug entirely.

What's in My Medicine?

Active ingredients in some common over-the-counter pain medications:

Brand Name	Active Ingredient
Advil	200 mg ibuprofen
Aleve	220 mg naproxen sodium
Anacin	400 mg aspirin, 32 mg caffeine
Bayer	325 mg aspirin
Bayer Extra Strength	500 mg aspirin
Bufferin	325 mg aspirin*
Bufferin Extra Strength	500 mg aspirin*
Ecotrin, regular strength	325 mg aspirin**
Excedrin	250 mg acetaminophen, 250 mg aspirin, 65 mg caffeine
Excedrin Migraine	250 mg acetaminophen, 250 mg aspirin, 65 mg caffeine
Excedrin Tension Headache	500 mg acetaminophen, 65 mg caffeine
Motrin	200 mg ibuprofen
St. Joseph	81 mg aspirin
Tylenol Regular Strength	325 mg acetaminophen
Tylenol Extra Strength	500 mg acetaminophen
Vanquish	227 mg aspirin, 194 mg acetaminophen, 33 mg caffeine

*Buffered with calcium carbonate, magnesium oxide, and magnesium carbonate
**Enteric-coated (absorbed mainly in the small intestine rather than in the stomach)

Opioids: For When Something Stronger Is Needed. If milder analgesics, NSAIDs, and other therapies don't provide sufficient relief, your doctor may suggest opioids, a large class of potent painkilling drugs that includes morphine and other medications. Formerly called "narcotics," *opioids* is the preferred term now. An opiate is any drug derived from the opium poppy (*Papaver somniferum*). Morphine and codeine are examples of opiates. Your body also produces natural opioids.

The most commonly prescribed opioids for acute back pain are codeine or semisynthetic compounds related to codeine such as oxycodone or hydrocodone. Moderate pain is often treated with medications that combine an opioid with another class of drug: oxycodone with aspirin (Percodan) or acetaminophen (Percocet); codeine with acetaminophen (Tylenol III); hydrocodone with acetaminophen (Vicodin). These combinations make it possible to use lower dosages of each drug. This can help minimize the potential side effects of each while still delivering effective pain relief. For instance, if drug A affects the kidneys and drug B the liver, by taking 50 percent lower doses of the two drugs as a combination dose rather than the full amount of one or the other, you lower the risk of harming the kidneys or liver by 50 percent.

Because opioids mimic the body's natural painkilling chemicals, they are capable of providing better relief than any other type of medication. However, some doctors and patients are hesitant about using opioids. Some worry about the legal issues surrounding these powerful substances; others are concerned about the possibility of becoming addicted. While it is true that when opioids are used over longer periods for ongoing chronic back pain, behavioral problems can occasionally develop, this is unusual. Opioids can, however, have some troublesome side effects. These vary from drug to drug, but may include constipation, sedation, slower breathing, and suppression of the coughing reflex. Elderly patients tend to be more sensitive to opioids. For these reasons, opioids are usually used for a limited time to treat acute back pain; chronic, unrelenting back pain

The OxyContin Story

You've no doubt read of the rash of criminal activities around the painkiller OxyContin, including robberies of pharmacies carrying the medication. OxyContin is a formulation of the pain medication oxycodone, an opioid that's similar to morphine. When a pill is swallowed whole, as it is designed, OxyContin is slowly and steadily released into the body over a twelve-hour period. Spurred by reports of the drug's effectiveness, pain specialists and general practitioners alike began prescribing OxyContin with increasing frequency. Drug abusers, however, quickly discovered that by crushing the tablets, they could create a powder that produces an immediate and intense high. Aided by the Internet, word of this relatively easy-to-obtain medication traveled quickly. Before long, OxyContin was the pill of choice on the street.

Alarmed by the trend of abuse, yet concerned that tighter controls might prevent legitimate patients from having access to the medication, the drug manufacturer and several federal agencies banded together to develop strategies for thwarting illicit use. Measures put in place so far include discontinuing the highest dose pills (160 mg), issuing warnings to health-care professionals about the abuse potential of OxyContin, and requiring prescription holders to preorder their medication so that pharmacies don't need to keep large quantities of the drug on the premises. The manufacturer is also researching ways to alter the drug's opioid effect if the tablet were to be crushed.

that has failed to respond to other treatments; and for pain control following back surgery. See Table 6.2 for a list of opioids commonly prescribed to treat more severe acute and chronic back pain.

Table 6.2
Opioids: The Stronger Pain Medications

Drug Name	Brand Name	Comments
Codeine	Generic formulations	Often combined with Tylenol. Perhaps the most commonly prescribed pain medication. Has a ceiling effect: dosages greater than 60 mg have no additional painkilling benefit. Usual dose is 15–60 mg every four hours. Used for mild to moderate pain resulting from a variety of causes, such as injury and surgery.
Fentanyl	Duragesic patch	Related to meperidine. 75–125 times more potent than morphine for temporary pain and 30–40 times more potent for persistent pain. Unlike morphine, does not cause histamine release, which can cause allergic reactions and other side effects. Fentanyl citrate is used for anesthesia during operations. Can be given via skin patches because it is highly fat-soluble. Fentanyl patches deliver tiny doses at a rate of 25–100 micrograms (mcg) per hour.
Hydromorphone	Dilaudid	A derivative of morphine but about five times more potent. Slightly shorter duration. Safe for patients with kidney problems. Oral, rectal, and injectable formulations are available. Usual oral dose is 2 mg every four to six hours.

(continued)

Table 6.2

Opioids: The Stronger Pain Medications continued

Drug Name	Brand Name	Comments
Meperidine	Demerol	Available as a syrup or in an injectable form. Far less effective when taken orally. Short duration of action; lasts about three hours. High and frequently repeated doses are dangerous and may cause seizures. Potentially fatal if given to patients on the antidepressants known as MAO inhibitors. Usual dose is 50–100 mg every three hours.
Methadone	Dolophine	Used as a maintenance drug for people addicted to opioids. Also used to treat severe pain. Stays active in the body longer than other opioids. Side effects of sedation and slowed breathing outlast pain-relieving effects.
Morphine	Kadian, MS Contin, Oramorph	Can be taken in many forms: by mouth, as a rectal suppository, through injection, or through catheters threaded into spaces surrounding the spinal cord. Due to liver metabolism, effectiveness declines by three to six times when taken orally. Small amounts of morphine given through catheters threaded into spaces of the spine can produce profound pain relief that lasts 12–24 hours. Usual dose of immediate-release oral morphine is 10–30 mg every four hours, but dosages vary widely depending on the route of administration. Long-acting formulations last 12–24 hours. MS Contin is a sustained-release formula created by covering morphine granules with a waxy coating.

Drug Name	Brand Name	Comments
Oxycodone	OxyContin, Percocet, Percodan, Roxicet, Roxicodone, Tylox	Semisynthetic compound related to codeine. Roxicodone and OxyContin are oxycodone alone; Percodan is oxycodone combined with aspirin; Percocet, Roxicet, and Tylox are oxycodone combined with acetaminophen. Effective when taken orally. OxyContin has high abuse potential because it is quickly absorbed into the bloodstream when crushed. This produces a rapid "high." Used to treat pain after injury or surgery. Dosages vary.
Propoxyphene	Darvocet, Darvon, Darvon Compound	Darvon is propoxyphene alone; Darvocet is propoxyphene combined with acetaminophen; Darvon Compound is propoxyphene combined with aspirin and caffeine. Usual dose is 50–100 mg every four hours. Used for mild pain.
Tramadol	Ultram	A semisynthetic opiate; has effects and toxicities similar to other opiates. About 15% less potent than codeine. Usefulness as postoperative drug still being researched. Usual dose is 50–100 mg every four to six hours.

Muscle Relaxants. Muscle relaxants are no better than standard NSAIDs for treating the symptoms of most acute back pain. However, a short course of a muscle relaxant such as cyclobenzaprine (Flexeril) or baclofen (Lioresal) can be useful for people who have severe muscle spasms at the onset of a back-pain episode. Carisoprodol (Soma) and methocarbamol (Robaxin) are also helpful for some people. A short course of the tranquilizer diazepam (Valium), a member of the benzodiazepine group of medicines, is sometimes used to relax muscles and relieve muscle spasms.

Low-Dose Antidepressants for Chronic Back Pain. People with persistent back pain, particularly those suffering from nerve pain, can benefit from antidepressants. While people with ongoing pain often get depressed and take an antidepressant medication to relieve their depression, these drugs also have an independent effect on pain sensation by increasing the levels of serotonin and norepinephrine, neurotransmitters that ratchet down pain signals.

The antidepressants most commonly used for pain treatment are the tricyclics. This category includes amitriptyline (Elavil, Endep), nortriptyline (Aventyl, Pamelor), desipramine (Norpramin), and imipramine (Tofranil). When used for nerve pain, tricyclics relieve pain at just one-half to one-third of the dose needed for depression. They also work faster for pain than they do for depression. The chief drawback of tricyclic antidepressants is their side effects: drowsiness, dry mouth, and weight gain. They also may blur vision and impair memory. I tend to use antidepressants if patients are having difficulty sleeping because of back pain and if they have tingling and burning, as these symptoms are most responsive to antidepressants.

Anticonvulsants. These drugs treat seizure disorders, but they're also used for several types of nerve-related pain, including cervical and lumbar pinched nerve syndromes, and neck and back pain resulting from shingles. Researchers aren't sure how anticonvulsants relieve pain, but some theorize that they work by interfering with nerve cell signaling. The anticonvulsants most frequently used for pain relief include gabapentin (Neurontin), carbamazepine (Tegretol), and clonazepam (Klonopin). Gabapentin is often the first anticonvulsant used for nerve pain because it has fewer side effects than the others. While these drugs are clearly effective in nerve disorders such as shingles and diabetic neuropathy, their effectiveness in sciatic pain and low-back pain is less well established. I occasionally offer these medications to patients with sciatic pain but discontinue them if patients don't find them helpful.

Combinations for Severe Pain

Pain treatment is developing rapidly. There is evolving evidence that pain medications are effective in combinations. Many experts in the field use more than one medication to treat severe pain. One drug is typically an analgesic; for severe pain this is often an opiate. Other medications are used as adjuncts, to address the multiple pain mechanisms. Thus, an opiate such as oxycodone is often given in a regimen that also includes gabapentin (Neurontin) or amitriptyline, as well as acetaminophen and perhaps an NSAID.

The Golden Rule of Pain Control

The best pain control is achieved when the medication, whatever its classification, is taken on a regular schedule rather than after the pain flares up. Practicing pain control is a bit like fighting a brush fire: it's better to intervene when the problem is just smoldering. Once it flares up, it's much harder to damp down again. You end up playing catch-up with the pain level. Living with pain is not a test of stamina. If you are experiencing discomfort, get comfortable, and let the healing begin!

Other Pain Medicine Delivery Methods

Up to now I've primarily discussed OTC and prescription medications as taken orally. You swallow a pill; its contents are released as part of the body's digestive process; the pharmacologically active chemicals enter the bloodstream and eventually interact with the nervous system. This is quite a journey, and a somewhat inefficient one, as some of the medication may not be absorbed and may not reach the target tissues.

But medications can be administered in other ways. People who become nauseous when taking oral medications, especially higher doses of opioids, are sometimes prescribed an opioid skin patch (Fentanyl, for example). Medication released from the patch enters the bloodstream directly, bypassing the wasteful digestive process and ensuring that more of the medicine is available to be taken up by the peripheral nervous system.

Another strategy is to deliver medications locally, not via the bloodstream. For some problems that occur near the skin, such as a sore muscle, a topical cream might be helpful. A number of OTC and prescription creams (Zostrix, for example) contain capsaicin, the chemical found in chili peppers, which interrupts the pain signaling pathway from the sore spot to the brain. Topical anesthetics such as lidocaine (Lidoderm) are also effective for localized, surface back pain.

For deeper-seated problems, injections of medications into the target tissues can temporarily relieve pain. This strategy has given rise to the field of interventional pain management.

Interventional Pain Management. One of the most rapidly growing fields in pain control is the use of injection therapies and other specialized treatments to treat pain at its source. Collectively termed interventional pain management, these techniques are performed by radiologists, pain specialists, neurosurgeons, or other medical specialists to target the precise points in the nervous or musculoskeletal systems that are at the root of the distress. Although there are many specific treatments (based on the nerve or joint involved and the type of medication used), injection therapies fall into some basic groups: blocks using local anesthetics, steroid injections, and trigger point injections. Other specialized pain treatments include procedures that use electrical current to stimulate certain nerves, procedures to destroy pain-causing nerves or tissue, and techniques to cement fractures of the vertebrae. I talk about these last two in Chapter 9, when I discuss surgical options for back pain.

Interventional pain management may be useful for certain types of low-back and neck pain. However, these techniques are not suitable for everyone. The length of time the pain has been present, the person's response to medication, the existence of other medical conditions, and the skill of the doctor performing the procedure all influence the success of the treatment.

Although these therapies can stand alone, they are often used in conjunction with other treatments. For example, injection of an anesthetic can make it possible to exercise, thereby hastening the rehabilitation process. I favor this approach of using injections as part of a broader strategy to treat a back-pain problem. The strategy should generally include exercise, as patients with severe and/or chronic back pain develop muscle atrophy and weakness. Exercise is very helpful in this situation.

Nerve Blocks. Nerve block injections are designed to interrupt pain signals as they travel to the brain. Using current imaging technologies, doctors can block virtually any nerve in the body. In some cases, a single injection or a series of injections of a local anesthetic can head off persistent pain and eliminate the need for medications for long periods of time. In other cases, numbing an area with a nerve block is sometimes helpful in permitting more progress in physical therapy. Exactly why a nerve block can work in such a way is unclear, but one theory is that the temporary blockade of nerve signals quells the constant bombardment of pain signals and allows the exaggerated pain sensitivity to subside.

Nerve blocks serve diagnostic as well as therapeutic purposes. Let's think about sciatica. Using imaging techniques and other diagnostic tests, your doctor may have determined that you have several bulging disks in your spine but may not know which of these is impinging on the sciatic nerve and causing your leg pain. By taking a trial-and-error approach to injecting an anesthetic into each of the nerves potentially involved, your doctor can eventually isolate the specific nerve that's causing your discomfort. This paves the way for additional therapeutic nerve blocks or other targeted treatments such as surgery.

Short-acting nerve blocks rely on injecting a local anesthetic like lidocaine or marcaine. Longer-acting nerve blocks, which last for several months, usually involve the injection of alcohol, a similar chemical called "phenol," cold (cryoanalgesia), or heat (radio-frequency lesioning), which kill nerve cells. Nerve blocks can relieve both temporary and persistent pain; and they can be useful in treating whiplash, headaches stemming from damage to a nerve at the base of the skull, and chronic low-back pain resulting from a pinched nerve. But no nerve block is permanent; eventually the relief wears off.

Steroid Injections. Glucocorticoids, commonly referred to as "steroids," are powerful anti-inflammatory agents. Although they can be taken orally, doctors sometimes inject steroids to treat back pain. These are different from the steroids some athletes take to bulk up, but they are not without risk. Three important considerations around the use of steroids are: they can destroy cartilage, they can make bones more brittle, and they can depress the function of the immune system.

Epidural Steroid Injections. Epidural steroid injections are not suitable for everyone with back pain, but they may benefit people who are suffering sharp, shooting nerve-compression pain, such as sciatica, as long as the treatment is done within three months after the symptoms begin. Within this time frame, studies have reported that 70 to 80 percent of people with acute sciatic pain experience an improvement in their symptoms. But even in these cases, the epidural injection is not a cure per se, but rather a way to relieve pain while the back heals naturally. This course of treatment doesn't seem to benefit people with long-standing back or neck pain.

Epidural steroid injections are typically done on an outpatient basis by a skilled specialist who injects the medication into the epidural space, an area that lies outside the spinal cord (see Figure 6.3). Although some of the steroid medication injected into the epidural space spreads to other parts of the body, the amounts are small, and complications from epidural steroid injections are rare. You usually feel some relief one to seven days after the first injection. Typically, more than one injection is needed.

Before undergoing epidural injections, keep several things in mind. First, such injections are not proven remedies for all types of back pain, but only stopgap pain relief measures for some types. In particular, they are generally useful for nerve root compression syndromes, for example, disk herniation and spinal stenosis. They usually are *not* useful for the common sprain-and-strain syndromes. A second consideration is that epidural injections can be quite painful and they do have complications, albeit rarely. (As with many medical interventions, there's no free lunch!) Third, the injections don't last forever. Even a very successful epidural injection typically lasts less than six months. Of course, if the syndrome gets better eventually, one good injection may be all that is needed to settle down the pain until the natural history of the condition plays out and the pain goes away.

Local Steroid Injections. In these procedures, your doctor injects steroids directly into the part of your back that is producing pain.

A. Epidural steroid injection

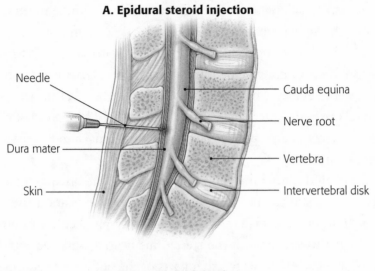

Needle

Dura mater

Skin

Cauda equina

Nerve root

Vertebra

Intervertebral disk

B. Facet joint injection

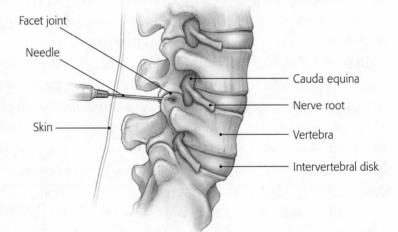

Facet joint

Needle

Skin

Cauda equina

Nerve root

Vertebra

Intervertebral disk

Figure 6.3

A Look at Two Steroid Injection Therapies

(A) Epidural steroid injections are used to treat back and neck pain. For this therapy, the doctor injects steroid medications into the epidural space. This area lies outside the dura mater, a membrane that covers the spinal cord. (B) When back pain is caused by an irritated facet joint, a doctor may suggest treating the problem with an injection of a steroid combined with a local anesthetic. Known as a "facet joint injection," this therapy delivers medication directly into the affected joint.

Let's be careful to distinguish these localized injections from the epidural injections I've just discussed, which are injected into the epidural space to reduce inflammation around irritated nerve roots. Localized steroid injections are sometimes used to treat persistent soft-tissue back pain such as tendonitis (inflammation of a tendon), tenosynovitis (inflammation of the lining of a tendon sheath), bursitis (inflammation of the saclike cavities that allow tendons or muscles to slide easily over bone), and occasionally cases of pinched nerve syndrome. (It's not uncommon for professional athletes to receive steroid shots to alleviate pain.) Often the steroid is mixed with a local anesthetic such as lidocaine. Just how effective local steroid injections are is not known. There is also some concern that while these shots dampen inflammation, in the long run they may potentially interfere with the healing process and weaken tendons.

Facet Joint Injections. Remember the facet joints located between the vertebrae that can become irritated and a source of back pain? Doctors can successfully treat this irritation by injecting a combination of a local anesthetic, such as lidocaine, and a steroid into the joint (see Figure 6.3). One thing to consider, however, is that repeated exposure to steroids may carry the risk of destroying cartilage in the treated joints.

Trigger Point Injections. Trigger points are tender, irritable spots in muscles that trigger pain when touched. You may also feel pain in other parts of the body when a trigger point is touched. For example, a trigger point just behind the left ear refers pain to the left upper trapezius muscle that crosses the back of your shoulders. (The trapezius muscle is a common source of cervical pain.) Trigger points are the hallmarks of a painful condition called *myofascial pain syndrome*, which some doctors believe is an underdiagnosed source of back pain.

While experts don't know exactly how trigger point injections relieve pain, the procedure offers many patients relief. The standard treatment involves injecting a local anesthetic agent, such as lidocaine or bupivacaine, but some doctors simply insert needles or inject a saline solution. Injections of botulinum toxin (BOTOX) are also used to reduce muscle spasms.

An alternative to trigger point injections is the "spray and stretch" method whereby the muscle with the trigger point is soothed with a cooling spray of topical anesthetic. A physical therapist then stretches that muscle out to its fullest extent.

Electrical Stimulation Therapies

Pain is powered by electrochemical impulses relaying the pain message. It's logical then that disrupting the "electronics" of pain could influence pain relief. A number of pain-relief therapies adopt this approach.

Transcutaneous Electrical Nerve Stimulation (TENS)

TENS, which is used to treat low-back pain, employs low-voltage electrical current to induce pain relief (see Figure 6.4). The current is transmitted through electrodes that are taped to the skin, often near the area of the body that hurts. The electrodes are attached to a power unit about the size of a cellular phone. When muscle or back pain is being treated, the operator places the electrodes around the trigger point. The length of the treatment varies depending on the individual's needs, although a typical session might run about half an hour.

TENS is based on the gate control theory of pain I discussed earlier in this chapter. According to this theory, the low-voltage

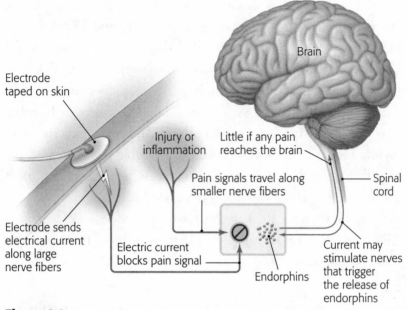

Brain

Electrode
taped on skin

Injury or
inflammation

Little if any pain
reaches the brain

Pain signals travel along
smaller nerve fibers

Spinal
cord

Electrode sends
electrical current
along large
nerve fibers

Electric current
blocks pain signal

Endorphins

Current may
stimulate nerves
that trigger
the release of
endorphins

Figure 6.4

How TENS Works

With transcutaneous electrical nerve stimulation (TENS), electrodes are placed
near the area of the body that hurts. TENS combats pain by instigating the gate
control theory of pain, whereby pain signals are garbled and blocked from reaching
the brain. TENS may also trigger the release of endorphins.

electric current prevents pain signals traveling through small
nerve fibers from reaching the brain by stimulating larger fibers
that "close the gate" in the spinal cord. Some TENS devices combine low- and high-frequency currents. The reasoning is that
the high-frequency current shuts the "pain gate," while the low-
frequency current stimulates pain-carrying nerve fibers, resulting
in the release of endorphins, the body's natural painkillers. TENS
devices are easy to use, can be purchased for at-home use, and
have minimal, if any, side effects.

Although people have been using TENS for decades, studies of its effectiveness have produced mixed results. Does TENS

work? The answer is a tentative maybe, but only for some people. A small British study comparing acupuncture and TENS among older people with back pain concluded that both treatments had benefits that outlasted a four-week treatment period. This was partly because some of the study participants bought and used TENS devices after the set treatment period was over. In other larger studies, TENS has not fared well, and many experts chalk up any benefits to a placebo effect, or what happens when people start feeling better simply by virtue of receiving medical treatment even if the particular treatment has no value.

If you have a pacemaker, check with your doctor before trying TENS because this therapy may interfere with the functioning of some pacemakers.

Percutaneous Electrical Nerve Stimulation (PENS)

PENS is a variation of TENS that uses acupuncture-like needles to deliver the electrical current under the skin. ("Percutaneous" means passing through the skin.) Proponents of PENS say it works better than TENS because the electrical stimulus is delivered closer to nerve endings.

Spinal Cord Stimulation

Another approach to treating chronic back pain caused by a pinched nerve syndrome is spinal cord stimulation. The procedure was originally developed on the premise that pain can be overcome by stimulating parts of the nervous system not normally involved in pain transmission. It now seems that spinal cord stimulation also releases neurotransmitters that block pain.

A spinal cord stimulator consists of a pulse generator attached by leads to four to eight electrodes implanted along the spinal column. In some models, the pulse generator is entirely implantable and runs on a non-rechargeable battery that will need replacing at some point. In others, it connects with an external power source via a radio-frequency antenna and transmitter carried outside the body and an implanted receiver. You can set the frequency, intensity, and duration of the electrical pulses using a small remote-control device.

Before having a spinal cord stimulator permanently implanted, you must undergo a trial in which a temporary device is implanted for a few days to see if the therapy will work for you. A successful test period—measured by at least a 50 percent reduction in pain, less need for pain medication, and improved function—is followed by a surgical procedure to implant the permanent device. You shouldn't consider this approach to pain control until you've exhausted all the other less invasive pain-control approaches and if surgery is not likely to help your back disorder. People with pacemakers can't have spinal stimulation therapy because it would disrupt their pacemakers.

None of us functions when all we can think about is pain. In this chapter we've discussed traditional ways of managing pain. In Chapter 7 we discuss complementary therapies. Above all, you need to be comfortable for the healing and rehabilitation to begin.

Chapter : 7

Can Complementary Therapies Help Your Aching Back?

When used in conjunction with mainstream medicine, some complementary therapies can help in the treatment of back pain. To obtain the best benefits from complementary medicine, however, takes investigative effort on the part of patient and doctor alike and a good, open relationship between the patient and his or her doctor. Let me begin by telling you about one of my patients who exemplifies a successful blending of complementary and conventional medicine.

Phil is a fifty-year-old professional with chronic back pain. I've worked with Phil for more than a decade, but his problems started years before in early adulthood. Phil has congenital lumbar stenosis—a narrowing of the spinal column that leads to painful nerve compression. By the time I met him, Phil had undergone three surgeries, taken all sorts of medications, and undergone injection therapies. But his pain persisted. Phil is an inquisitive, open-minded man. As we discussed his situation, he expressed interest in trying a range of different therapies, some conventional, some complementary. He was especially interested in Eastern medicine approaches. I encouraged Phil to check out acupuncture. It helped considerably with his pain. Phil and I have now settled on a regimen of opiate medications, occasional epidural and trochanteric bursa injections, and acupuncture treatments. This mélange of East and West, ancient and modern, low-tech and high-tech, is perfectly comfortable for Phil—and for me as well.

You may not have put up with back pain for as long as Phil, but unless you're having an episode of garden-variety sprain and strain, which will be gone in a matter of days or weeks, you may be facing (or have already endured) weeks to months of nagging or even sharp back pain. The medications and pain treatments I described in the previous chapter help to control longer-lasting pain, but people with chronic back pain often seek out unconventional, complementary, and alternative therapies. According to a 2003 survey by Harvard Medical School researchers at Beth Israel Deaconess Medical Center in Boston, one-third of all visits to complementary medicine providers are for the treatment of back or neck pain. Some patients with back pain embrace complementary medicine in the hope of finding further relief from their nagging condition; some are plainly dissatisfied with conventional treatments; others have the expectation that by adding complementary therapies to their traditional treatment regimens, they'll be able to cut back on the amount of pharmacological medication they're taking. Certainly several complementary therapies can go some way to meeting these expectations; and numerous hospitals, pain clinics, and physical therapists have added alternative therapies to their repertoires. In the United States, the three complementary therapies most often used to treat back pain are spinal manipulation, massage, and acupuncture. When I discuss complementary therapies with my patients, I indicate that I think these treatments can be beneficial when used in conjunction with conventional therapies, but my endorsement comes with a number of caveats.

Many complementary or alternative therapies, such as massage, yoga, acupuncture, and meditation, are not likely to cause harm and seem to help some back-pain patients. At least they seem to help for a while, which is no small accomplishment for patients in the grip of persistent pain. There have been good scientific studies of some complementary therapies. But for many others, science has yet to determine just how effective they are as back-pain treatments. Another consideration is that even harmless therapies can be harmful if they're administered incorrectly. And some therapies may be dangerous for certain types of back pain. Chiropractic manipulation, for instance, is generally safe and effective for garden-variety lower-back strain but can be dangerous when applied to a pinched nerve case, especially in the neck. Consequently, you should approach certain therapies with caution, depending on the type of back pain you have and where your back problem is in its natural healing process.

You should also discuss any therapies you are considering with your doctor. My advice is that you pause to consider and confer before uncritically embracing complementary therapies simply because they seem to be more "natural" and have fewer side effects. (An exception to this advice is meditation, which is not harmful and can be very beneficial whether you do—or don't—have back pain.) Like everything having to do with back pain, getting the latest update and seeing how it applies to your individual circumstances is what matters. If you're considering using a complemen-

Keeping the Names Straight

For back-pain therapy there's traditional, or Western, medicine and then there's everything else. For those therapies that fall into the "everything else" category, several terms are bandied about interchangeably, which can be confusing. Here's a rundown of the common terms you're likely to hear:

- **Conventional medicine**, sometimes referred to as "Western," "traditional," "standard," or "mainstream" medicine, is medicine as practiced by a licensed medical doctor (M.D.), or a doctor of osteopathy (D.O.) who has a medical degree from an accredited osteopathic medical school. Some of these doctors may also practice complementary and alternative medicine. Examples of conventional medicine are medication and surgery.

- **Alternative medicine** means precisely what it says: therapies that are administered as alternatives to conventional medicine. Alternative medicines are systems and practices of healing independent of conventional Western medicine. They typically predate Western medicine. An example would be if you relied exclusively on a traditional Eastern medicine such as acupuncture to treat your back-pain problem.

- **Complementary medicine**, as its name suggests, complements conventional medicine. An example is a back-pain patient who is taking a prescription pain medication and undergoing a course of acupuncture at the same time, such as my patient Phil.

    Sometimes you'll hear complementary medicine referred to as "complementary/alternative medicine" (CAM), meaning a combination of complementary and alternative medicine. While you may see "complementary" and "alternative" used interchangeably, they are not the same. Some therapies, such as acupuncture, are part of an alternative medicine system, yet can also be used as a complementary therapy. Used alone, acupuncture is an alternative therapy. Used in conjunction with traditional approaches, acupuncture is a complementary therapy. It's easy to see how the terminology can be confusing.

- **Complementary/integrative medicine (CIM)** combines conventional medicine and complementary approaches into a single treatment plan that equally recognizes and uses the best of both. This approach can be especially helpful for persistent back pain that has not been relieved by conventional medicine alone or when the patient prefers a "wait-and-watch" approach before deciding to have surgery.

tary therapy, be sure to be fully informed as to its efficacy and safety record when applied to your back disorder. To point you in the right direction, in this chapter I'll be discussing the various complementary therapies commonly used in the treatment of back pain.

Get the Best: Is Your Therapist Qualified?

When you visit your primary care doctor, you can be confident you are visiting a professional who graduated from an accredited medical school and then went on to serve a professional "apprenticeship" as a resident in a hospital for some number of years. When you seek out a complementary therapist, you don't necessarily have such guarantees. Yet you need to know that the person you are consulting is knowledgeable and competent should you decide to go ahead with a course of therapy. Fortunately, you're not left totally floundering. There are a couple of safeguards. In the United States, many states have mandatory licensing or registration requirements for some therapies; and professional organizations have standards for membership. Similarly, in other countries—the United Kingdom and Canada, for instance—national professional organizations have registries of therapists. If you're considering a complementary therapist, you should ask about credentials and professional affiliations. Don't be bashful. A bona fide therapist would expect you to check him or her out.

If you have a question about a particular therapy or wonder which therapy would be appropriate in your situation, a good place to start is the National Center for Complementary and Alternative Medicine (NCCAM), a center within the National Institutes of Health (NIH) of the U.S. government and an invaluable online resource (nccam.nih.gov). NCCAM is "dedicated to exploring complementary and alternative healing practices in the context of rigorous science." For readers who reside in other countries, you might want to refer to the online medical sites of your country of residence's health-care provider, such as the National Health System in the United Kingdom.

Now let's consider the various therapies.

Spinal Manipulation

"Spinal manipulation," an old, yet controversial, treatment for pain, is sometimes used as a generic term for any kind of therapeutic movement of the spine. It's the core technique of chiropractic medicine. And osteopathic medicine, which has been folded into mainstream medicine, is also based on theories about the benefit of spinal manipulation for restoring blood flow. Today, osteopathy is part of conventional physical therapy for low-back pain. Chiropractic manipulation, however, which accounts for 90 percent of spinal manipulation visits, is a complementary (when used with mainstream approaches) or alternative therapy—albeit one that is licensed in all American states.

Chiropractic Manipulation

Spinal manipulation as used in chiropractic medicine is the application of quick, strong pressure on a joint between two vertebrae of the spine. The pressure twists or rotates the joint beyond its normal range of motion. It may cause a sharp, cracking noise, which is why people talk about chiropractors "cracking the spine." This hands-on manipulation of the spine is also called "adjustment." The "cracking" noise appears to reflect the breaking of a vacuum or the release of a bubble into the synovial fluid—the clear, thick fluid that lubricates spinal and other joints. These processes are both considered harmless by-products of the treatment. The manipulation can either be done directly, by pushing on one of the vertebrae, or indirectly, by twisting the neck or upper part of the body. It should be done to only one spinal joint at a time. Chiropractors accomplish that by positioning the body so the force they exert is focused on one joint while parts of the spine above and below that joint are held still.

Spinal manipulation is usually safe, but it should generally not be done as complementary treatment for pinched nerve syndromes. The technique may potentially be hazardous for the neck because manipulating the joints in this area carries some risk of injury to blood vessels or the spinal cord. In rare instances these injuries can cause death. The question hanging over the tech-

nique is whether it's effective, and if so, for what. Spinal manipulation appears to be beneficial in patients with low-back strain
and sprain. When my patients with garden-variety low-back pain
ask me about chiropractic treatment, I'm generally supportive. We
know less about the effectiveness of chiropractic in chronic low-
back pain and in disk protrusion and spinal stenosis syndromes.
I typically don't recommend chiropractic manipulation in these
situations, and I'm very cautious about the use of manipulation for
the neck.

Chiropractic: Not All It's Cracked Up to Be

Avoid chiropractic manipulation if you have osteoporosis or rheumatoid arthritis, or if you have neck pain that might stem from infection
or fracture. If you have neurological symptoms along with your lumbar or cervical pain—such as tingling or numbness, which suggests a
pinched nerve condition—you should probably not undergo chiropractic manipulation. Very rarely, chiropractic manipulations can worsen or
even cause disk herniation, nerve-root irritation, or spinal cord injury.
The neck is particularly vulnerable and at risk. Among the most serious and rare complications of chiropractic manipulation of the neck is
vertebral or carotid artery dissection, a tearing of the arteries supplying
blood to the brain, which can lead to stroke. Neurological symptoms
of this life-threatening condition may occur immediately or up to a
week or more after the adjustment. Experts advise that chiropractors
avoid one particular movement, called "rotational thrust," on the neck
and use no manipulation of the neck on people with serious degenerative disease.

Current Status of Spinal Manipulation

Several years ago, a U.S. government panel on back pain gave spinal manipulation a qualified endorsement, saying that spinal manipulation can relieve pain if a person has it done within the first month of symptoms. A 1999 study in the *New England Journal of Medicine* found that standard treatment (pain medication, anti-inflammatory drugs, muscle relaxants, and physical therapy) and osteopathic spinal manipulation had similar results for people with back pain, although those who received spinal manipulation needed less pain medication. Other studies have concluded that spinal manipulation doesn't work for tension headaches.

Massage

Another hands-on therapy is massage (see Figure 7.1). Although massage proponents have long claimed it provides pain relief, evidence to back up these claims has been slow in coming. There is little question that a properly done massage can make you feel better for a while. Many people find that massage reduces stress and lifts their spirits. For anyone who is in continual pain, that may be recommendation enough. And a massage followed by a warm soak in the tub leading to a good night's sleep is hard to beat. The difficult question has been whether massage has therapeutic benefits beyond this. At last, a well-designed review study published in the *Annals of Internal Medicine* in 2003 says yes, it does.

The investigators compiled data from forty-nine clinical trials on the effectiveness of massage, acupuncture, and spinal manipulation for the treatment of low-back pain. They concluded that of the three therapies, only massage had a clear benefit over conventional treatment in relieving pain and could potentially reduce the health-care cost associated with chronic back pain. In addition, a 2002 study demonstrated that massage of specific head and shoul-

Figure 7.1

Healing Hands of Massage

While we don't know exactly how it works, massage has been shown to effectively relieve some types of pain.

der muscles could reduce the frequency and duration of tension headaches.

Massage increases superficial circulation in the area being rubbed and can help loosen up tight muscles. But it's not entirely clear how the therapy works. While a variety of other benefits—such as increased endorphin levels, improved immune system, and healthful drainage of the lymphatic system—have been ascribed to massage, they haven't been proven. There is some speculation that massage works by way of the gate control theory, in which the stimulation of certain nerve fibers impedes the delivery of pain messages to the brain. I discuss this theory in Chapter 6.

How Do I Know What to Believe?

One of the difficulties of assessing the value of chiropractic—or other CAM techniques—is that many of the studies of CAM therapies were not sufficiently well designed to gather reliable scientific data. In an attempt to address this problem, a group of researchers sifted through the available material for reliable studies on which to base a conclusion. Their study findings, titled "A Review of the Evidence for the Effectiveness, Safety, and Cost of Acupuncture, Massage Therapy, and Spinal Manipulation for Back Pain," were published in the *Annals of Internal Medicine* in 2003.

For most people, massage is generally safe and worth a try. But there are certain situations in which massage can do more harm than good. Massaging an inflamed area or joint, for example, can make it worse by causing irritation. The American Massage Therapy Association recommends that people with certain heart problems, infectious disease, phlebitis, and some skin conditions forgo massage therapy.

Before trying massage, check the credentials of the massage therapist. Look for an experienced, properly certified practitioner, ideally someone who has experience with back-pain patients. Many states regulate massage therapists. Or ask the massage therapist if he or she has been certified by the National Certification Board for Therapeutic Massage and Bodywork.

Acupuncture

Acupuncture has been practiced for centuries in Asia but has become popular in the Western world only in recent decades. Although traditional Chinese medical acupuncture is the most prevalent method used in the United States and elsewhere, other forms of acupuncture are also practiced.

According to traditional Chinese medical beliefs, acupuncture works by affecting the flow of energy, called *qi* (pronounced chee), via pathways, called *meridians*, that run lengthwise through the body. Acupuncture needles are inserted into points along those meridians. Typically, four to ten needles are used and left in place for ten to thirty minutes. A typical course of treatment includes six to twelve sessions over a three-month period. The needles are extremely fine, and insertion of them doesn't hurt (See Figure 7.2).

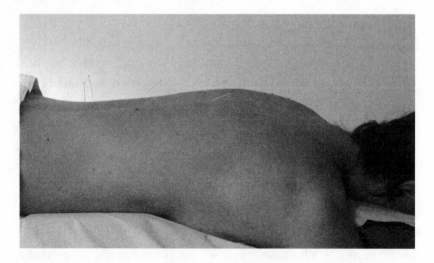

Figure 7.2

Acupuncture Appears to Benefit Some Back-Pain Patients

Acupuncture uses extremely fine needles. Inserting them doesn't hurt. Needles should be discarded after a one-time use.

Some research has shown that acupuncture needles provoke the release of the body's natural pain-stifling chemicals, which act on the same nerve cell receptors as morphine. Experiments have also shown that acupuncture has an effect on the part of the brain that governs levels of serotonin, a chemical that can interfere with the transmission of pain signals in the body. One interesting finding was that the techniques of acupuncture apparently help some patients even when the needles are not inserted along the traditional meridians. But the question remained: How effective is acupuncture for chronic back pain? This has been difficult to determine, because although there have been a number of studies, they have tended to be of poor quality. Until 2003, studies had very few subjects, making their results—pro or con—suspect. And the variations in skill and technique among acupuncture practitioners make comparisons between studies difficult. A 2003 study published in the *Annals of Internal Medicine* confirmed the inadequacy of previous studies. The authors of the study concluded that their review of past studies "did not clearly indicate that acupuncture is effective in the management of back pain." They went on to say that more high-quality trials are needed "before clinically meaningful conclusions could be reached." The jury, then, is still out on acupuncture and back pain—at least until there is more reliable scientific evidence. But some patients, such as my patient Phil, say it helps!

Variations of acupuncture are also used to treat back pain. Acupressure substitutes deep pressure (usually with a finger or thumb) for acupuncture needles, but it follows the same principle of affecting certain points in the body. Many mainstream pain clinics in hospitals use electroacupuncture, which involves sending a weak electrical current through metal acupuncture needles.

Acupuncture appears to be quite safe, and the complication rate is very low. To protect against blood-borne illnesses, be sure that the acupuncturist uses a new set of disposable needles at each appointment (a requirement of many U.S. states). And do your homework on the acupuncturist you intend to receive treatment from. Many U.S. states license acupuncturists. In states with no licensing requirements, an alternative is to seek out acupuncturists who have certification from the National Certification Commission for Acupuncture and Oriental Medicine. (Readers who reside in other countries should check with their countries' national organizations typically available on the Internet.)

Mind-Body Therapies

Ironically, the disparaging remark, "Oh, it's all in your head" is true in a sense—but not in the dismissive way it is sometimes said. In an earlier chapter I discussed how the perception of pain in the brain results in the pain sensation (you feeling pain). If the recognition of pain resides in the brain, wouldn't it make sense that therapies that somehow influence the brain would also influence your response to pain? This does indeed appear to be so with certain complementary therapies, although we're not always sure precisely how it happens. Since we know that stress plays a role in back pain, any technique that minimizes your stress level is likely to be beneficial. Mind-body medicine encompasses a variety of therapies, the benefits of which vary from individual to individual. You may have to try several before you find the combination that works for your temperament and suits your lifestyle. In the next section I describe some of the more popular mind-body therapies.

Relaxation Techniques

Relaxation techniques are commonly used as part of a multidisciplinary pain-management program for persistent back pain. There

are a wide variety of techniques and dozens of different philoso-
phies, but most have some basic themes in common.

First, persistent back pain can rob you of a sense of control
over your body and, thus, your life. Relaxation techniques can
help restore that sense of control, which in itself can make you
feel a great deal better. Second, some back-pain conditions may
be perpetuated or worsened when the body's normal fight-or-flight
response is triggered too easily or becomes stuck in the "on" position. A goal of many relaxation techniques and programs is to
turn off the fight-or-flight reaction and calm revved-up muscle,
metabolic, and hormonal responses. Essentially, since stress can
contribute to or exacerbate pain, relaxation techniques can alleviate pain by easing stress. Finally, relaxation techniques help activate the body's natural painkillers. Working through a complex
web of mind-body networks, relaxation techniques prompt the
release of natural chemicals such as endorphins and enkephalins,
which enhance mood, reduce pain perception, and stimulate some
immune system cells.

Many relaxation techniques, including deep breathing and
progressive muscle relaxation, are aimed at achieving a state of
profound rest and release, known as the "relaxation response."
According to Dr. Herbert Benson, a renowned mind-body
researcher at Harvard Medical School, the relaxation response
is the antidote to the fight-or-flight mechanism. Invoking the
relaxation response regularly can lead to lasting declines in high
blood pressure, a decrease in anxiety and depression, and general
improvement in the ability to cope with stress.

Breath of Life

Although we do it every minute of every day without thinking, we
can consciously harness the power of our breath for healing. Con-

scious, controlled breathing is a building block of many relaxation therapies. The Lamaze technique used by women in labor is an example of a well-known, pain-combating relaxation technique based on breathing. An essential aspect of breathing exercises is disciplining yourself to concentrate in a calm way on something

Breathing for Your Back

Breath focus, which is a form of meditation, is the foundation of many relaxation techniques. Breath focus can induce relaxation, and some people find it helps ease pain. Occasionally health problems such as congestive heart failure or respiratory ailments may make using this technique uncomfortable. If that's the case for you, don't use this technique.

The first step in practicing breath focus is to learn to breathe properly. Find a comfortable, quiet place to sit or lie down. Start by noting the difference between breathing normally and breathing deeply. First take a normal breath. Now try a deep, slow breath. The air coming in through your nose should move downward into your lower belly. Let your abdomen expand fully. Now breathe out through your mouth—or your nose, if that feels more natural. Alternate normal and deep breaths several times. Pay attention to how you feel when you inhale and exhale normally and again when you inhale and exhale deeply. Shallow breathing often feels tense and constricted, while deep breathing produces relaxation.

Now practice deep breathing for several minutes. Put one hand on your abdomen. Feel your hand rise about an inch each time you inhale and fall about an inch each time you exhale. Your chest will rise slightly, too, in concert with your abdomen. Remember to relax your belly so that each inhalation expands it fully. As you exhale slowly, let yourself sigh out loud.

Once you've taken the steps above, you can move on to regular practice of breath focus. As you sit or lie comfortably with your eyes closed, blend deep breathing with helpful imagery and a focus word or phrase that will help you relax. Imagine that the air you breathe in washes peace and calm into your body. As you breathe out, imagine that the air leaving your body carries tension and anxiety away with it. As you inhale, try saying this phrase to yourself: "Breathing in peace and calm." And as you exhale, say: "Breathing out tension and anxiety." Continue to breathe deeply in this manner. When you first start, ten minutes of breath focus is a reasonable goal. Gradually increase the time until your sessions are at least twenty minutes long.

• •

that is ordinarily taken for granted: the simple act of breathing in and out. You train yourself to focus on breathing more slowly and deeply than you would ordinarily.

Meditation

Like breathing focus, the meditative state is a building block for many relaxation therapies. A meditative state can be achieved in many ways. Essentially, it is a passive mental condition that is often described as "emptying your mind" of active thought. Meditation helps people with the psychological aspects of chronic back pain by breaking anxious and depressive thought patterns and restoring some sense of control over their condition.

One form of meditation used in pain clinics is called "mindfulness meditation." It involves erasing the past and the future from your mind and focusing just on the present moment. A different technique, concentration meditation, involves focusing on a certain body process or word to bring about the meditative state. Transcendental meditation involves repeating a suitable sound or word to help enter the meditative state. You may have to try more than one technique before you find the one that works for you.

Guided Imagery

Guided imagery, or visualization, can promote relaxation. While imagery is often touted as beneficial for people with a variety of illnesses, more study is needed before many of these claims can be confirmed or refuted. It has, however, been proven to lessen pain and the side effects of various drugs, including chemotherapy.

In one variation of this therapy, you mentally conjure up a soothing scene. The image you choose should be pleasurable or hold good memories for you. The place you visualize might be culled from memory—a childhood bed or a summer vacation spot—or may simply be imagined. In another variation, a therapist may ask you to create a visual image of the pain you are experiencing or the painful part of your back. He or she might ask how big the pain is, what color it is, and where it is specifically located. Again, it's helpful to paint as full a picture as possible. The idea behind this kind of visualization is to create some mental distance between physiological pain and its psychological aspects, which are broadly defined as "suffering." Some experts caution that a visual image of pain can be monstrous and overwhelming, so this technique must be used carefully.

A Guided Imagery Primer

When starting an imagery session, find a quiet place to sit and arrange your body as comfortably as possible. Clear your mind while taking deep, even breaths for several minutes and then conjure up an image that you find relaxing. This can be an actual or an imaginary place. Flesh out the scene by picturing yourself there.

What do you smell—pine needles, rain steaming off hot pavement, vanilla in a kitchen? What do you hear? Try to engage your senses. Drink in the sights, smells, and sounds. Concentrate on sensory pleasures: a cool breeze on your cheek, the scent of flowering trees, the crunch of gravel underfoot.

If intrusive thoughts crop up, accept them passively by observing them, and then try to return to the scene you've created. Practice for fifteen minutes or more. You may find it helpful to record a tape describing all that you envision to return to this spot again.

Progressive Muscle Relaxation

Relaxing muscles in sequence is a common relaxation technique. Often progressive muscle relaxation is coordinated with breathing; you tighten muscles as you inhale and then relax them as you exhale. When learning the technique, you may find it helpful to work with an expert; a book or audiotape may also provide the instruction you need.

Going It Alone with Progressive Muscle Relaxation

Start by closing your eyes and sitting peacefully in a chair for a few moments. Then follow these steps slowly, taking the time to feel the tension build and dissipate in each set of muscles.

- Make fists with your hands. Hold for 10 seconds, release, and relax for 20 seconds.

- Bend your elbows and press your arms firmly into your sides. Hold for 10 seconds, release, and relax for 20 seconds.

- Flex your feet by pointing your toes upward toward your head. Hold for 10 seconds, release, and relax for 20 seconds.

- Press your knees together, lifting your legs off the chair. Hold for 10 seconds, release, and relax for 20 seconds.

- Pull your stomach in toward your spine. Hold for 10 seconds, release, and relax for 20 seconds.

- Take a deep breath and hold it for 10 seconds. Feel the pressure in your chest. Release, and relax for 20 seconds.

- Lift your shoulders upward toward your ears. Feel the tension in your neck and back for 10 seconds. Release, and relax for 20 seconds.

- Pull your chin down toward your chest. Hold for 10 seconds, release, and relax for 20 seconds.

- Make your face frown by pulling your eyebrows down toward the center of your face. Feel the tension in your forehead for 10 seconds. Release, and relax for 20 seconds.

- Breathe normally for 10 breaths, saying the word "relax" to yourself with each breath. Feel the warmth and relaxation spread slowly from your feet upward through your legs, then into your abdomen and chest. Feel the warmth and relaxation extend gradually into your arms and hands, and finally into your neck and head.

Yoga

Westerners sometimes think of yoga as an exercise program only, but the practice of yoga combines exercise with mental focus achieved through yoga breathing techniques (pranayama). While the physical aspects of yoga may be beneficial, it may be the mind-body connection that is most beneficial for people with back pain. The problem has been that until December 2005 there was no reliable scientific evidence to support the opinion of an estimated more than 1 million Americans who use yoga practices as a treatment for back pain. In December 2005, however, the *Annals of Internal Medicine* published a randomized controlled trial titled "Comparing Yoga, Exercise, and a Self-Care Book for Chronic Low Back Pain." This trial concluded that viniyoga, a therapeutically oriented style of yoga, was an effective treatment for chronic low-back pain. The authors caution that other styles of yoga may not be suitable for back-pain patients. Specifically, Bikram (a rigorous practice performed in a hot, steamy environment) and vinyasa (a series of postures performed as a continuous flow of movement) may be too vigorous. Iyengar, with its emphasis on long-held postures, may also need to be modified for people with back pain. The authors also noted that for their trial they selected simple poses from viniyoga (a gentle, flowing practice adapted to meet individual abilities) and avoided others. The message then would seem to be that a certain style of yoga has proved to be safe and effective for chronic back pain, but even that style needs modification. Another proviso is that you should only work with a yoga teacher who has experience working with people who have back pain.

Tai Chi

Tai chi as practiced today for health purposes is an adaptation of the martial art form tai chi chuan. Tai chi is designed to engage and benefit all parts of the body—not just the musculoskeletal system. Studies have documented the benefits of Tai chi in a number of populations, especially the elderly, in terms of improved balance, muscle tone, flexibility, and bone density. While Tai chi has not been studied carefully as a specific treatment for back pain, its benefits to overall health and well-being have been well documented.

Biofeedback: Measuring and Responding

Biofeedback, a popular trend of the 1960s and 1970s, can help relieve stress and pain. A machine measures pain- and stress-related levels of physiological functions such as temperature, blood pressure, and the electrical activity in muscles (a sign of muscle activity or tension). The machine translates those measurements into a blinking light, a beeping sound, or a graph (see Figure 7.3). Essentially, biofeedback lets you know when you're tensing a muscle, which can be both a cause and an effect of pain. A biofeedback therapist then teaches you relaxation exercises and thought patterns to change those signals. The result is supposed to be some conscious control of pain and stress.

The most common form of biofeedback has been the treatment of headache or back pain using surface electromyography (sEMG),

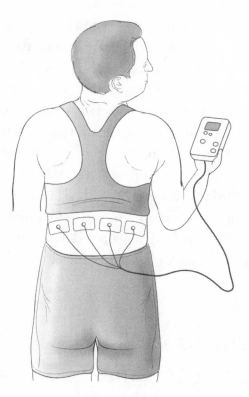

Figure 7.3

Understanding Biofeedback

Biofeedback helps people manage their own pain by relaying information about body responses, which the patient then brings under control. For lower-back pain, for example, heat sensors and electrodes painlessly record electrical activity and temperature. An instrument reports the results in the form of a blinking light, audible beep, or computer graph. The patient then uses relaxation techniques such as breathing exercises or meditation to slow or speed the blips to healthier frequencies. Portable devices (shown here) are available.

a measure of electrical activity in a muscle through electrodes placed on the skin. (The placement of electrodes on the skin in Figure 7.3 is an example of sEMG.) Biofeedback therapy usually begins with an instructional session with a nurse or therapist. Thereafter you may attend in-clinic sessions. Most proponents of biofeedback therapy say its effectiveness depends on regular, daily use of an at-home machine. As control over the targeted body functions increases, you're gradually weaned off the machine and instead use your newly acquired skills as needed. The therapist continues to monitor your progress but no longer directs treatment. A course of treatment usually lasts about three months.

Studies have found that biofeedback therapy can help people control headaches, back pain, and arthritis. A U.S. National Institutes of Health (NIH) expert panel endorsed biofeedback for the treatment of chronic pain in 1995, although the experts emphasized that it worked best when combined with standard pain relief medication. But as the NIH panel noted, following through on a full course of biofeedback is a big investment of time and money.

Complementary Exercise Programs

There are many complementary exercise programs available—the Alexander technique, Pilates, and so forth. (I briefly describe the Alexander technique and Pilates later.) Although not medically accredited programs, most of them are safe when conducted by a trained, experienced instructor. Indeed, as with any exercise program, it's essential you work only with a trained instructor, ideally someone experienced in back-pain disorders. Although the techniques may be helpful, in the wrong hands they can be harmful.

What are the differences between complementary exercise programs and conventional exercise programs? A major difference is not the exercise programs themselves—many of which have similarities—but that when you sign up for a complementary program, you're signing up for an "off the shelf" predesigned package. Yes, you could amend some of the exercises, as long as you know which ones you should amend. In contrast, when you work with a conventional physical therapist, the therapist typically designs a unique exercise program tailored to meet your specific needs. Another difference may be the beliefs that underlie the complementary exercises, which can lead to a particular emphasis on certain types of exercises. This is not necessarily wrong; just different. If you decide to sign up for a complementary exercise program, be sure you know what its emphasis is and whether that emphasis is suitable for your back condition. Before starting a program, I recommend checking with your doctor.

Here are a couple of popular complementary exercise programs—the Alexander technique and Pilates. I caution you that as of now the value of these techniques has either not been proven for back pain or the techniques are considered ineffective. Nonetheless, you may hear anecdotal stories about how these techniques brought relief when all else failed. If the techniques help you to feel better overall, then that sense of improved well-being can contribute positively to your recovery. There is little risk in trying, but you should not rely on these techniques alone to do the job of healing you.

Alexander Technique

The Alexander technique is a 100-year-old method designed to help you release patterns of tension in your muscles and connective tissue that may contribute to your pain and interfere with your freedom of movement. The idea is that as you let go of your acquired bad habits, over time you can learn to move with greater ease, placing less strain on your body. The basis of the technique is the release of muscular tension throughout the body. The technique also involves looking at balance, breathing, and posture.

While giving particular attention to your head and neck, the Alexander technique addresses how you use your whole body in daily activities. An Alexander teacher observes how habitual patterns of tension may cause or exacerbate your pain. Using light touch, verbal direction, and gently guided movements, the teacher helps you to notice and release any unnecessary tension. Instead of learning particular exercises or postures, you *undo* excessive muscle contraction that prevents you from sitting, standing, or moving with ease.

The Alexander technique is generally safe, but let your teacher know if you have a herniated disk or other condition that makes moving painful. In such cases, you may need to proceed more slowly and avoid certain types of movement. Many people report at least temporary relief—including diminished pain and increased range of motion—in just one or two sessions. However, changing deeply ingrained habits is a gradual process; it may take several months for you to experience lasting benefits. Very little clinical research has been done on the Alexander technique, so anecdotal claims are hard to verify scientifically. The Alexander technique is usually conducted in a group setting or one-on-one with a private teacher.

Pilates

Pilates is a method of exercise and physical movement designed to stretch, strengthen, and balance the body. The exercises, which are coupled with a pattern of focused breathing, are currently experiencing explosive popularity. Pilates classes are springing up everywhere, catering to people from every walk of life. Designed to be done on a mat or using specialized equipment, Pilates exercises are intended to increase the strength and flexibility of the muscles of the abdomen and back in particular.

The originator of the program, Joseph Pilates, insisted on a lengthy apprenticeship of two to three years before he allowed his instructors to teach. Today's instructors can receive Pilates certification in a matter of several weekends. My concern is that someone who has undergone such a short training period is far too inexperienced for you to entrust your problematic back to. If you do decide to give Pilates a try, make sure you work only with a seasoned instructor.

Other Complementary Pain Treatments

The Internet is a very useful resource for checking out CAM treatments—as long as you know how to use it. Just type *complementary* or *alternative* medicine into a search engine on your computer and you'll get a lot of hits. Be sure to thoroughly evaluate any therapies you are considering and who is sponsoring the site you are getting your information from. The official U.S. government website of the National Center for Complementary and Alternative Medicine (nccam.nih.gov) is an excellent research resource, as are the government sites of other countries.

Magnets

Magnets have long been touted as being able to relieve the pain of arthritis. All sorts of products using magnets are available, including mattress pads, pillows, and cushions. There is no reliable scientific evidence, however, that magnets live up to the claims of the manufacturers. According to NCCAM, the U.S. Food and Drug Administration (FDA) has not approved the marketing of magnets with attached health benefit claims such as "relieves arthritis pain." Furthermore, the FDA and the Federal Trade Commission (FTC) have taken action against many manufacturers, distributors, and websites that make claims about the health benefits of magnets that are not supported scientifically.

Music and Laughter

Although there's little hard evidence on whether or how music and laughter can combat pain, it's clear that neither can cause you any harm. Both activities offer simple ways to enrich your life—and if your pain is reduced in the process, all the better.

The adage "Laughter is the best medicine" may, however, be sound medical advice. Researchers believe that laughter may promote the release of endorphins, which blunt the sensation of pain. In addition, watching a funny movie or reading a humorous book is a pleasant way to distract yourself from physical discomfort. And being able to find humor in yourself and the world around you is important in maintaining a positive attitude and coping with your back pain.

Glucosamine and Chondroitin Sulfate Supplements

In recent years there's been much debate about the supplements glucosamine (pronounced glue-COSE-a-mean) and chondroitin (pronounced con-DROY-tin) sulfate to treat joint pain from arthritis. Advocates claim that glucosamine can help create and repair cartilage, while chondroitin sulfate can help give cartilage its elasticity. Sold as dietary supplements, these substances are touted as being able to relieve the joint pain of osteoarthritis and to halt and even reverse its progression. But the only studies to back up these claims were short-term, included relatively few patients, or had other flaws. More important, for back-pain sufferers these studies did not include back pain. Essentially there is no evidence that these supplements help painful back conditions.

As this book is being written, a large and well-done NIH-sponsored study has been published showing that glucosamine and chondroitin are not effective in mild knee osteoarthritis. The study, published in the *New England Journal of Medicine* in 2006, opined that the supplements may be beneficial in moderate-to-severe pain, but more studies are necessary to prove this. For back-pain sufferers, however, it's critical to understand that all the glucosamine and chondroitin studies have focused on *knee* osteoarthritis. There have been no studies of these agents in patients with back pain. Because back pain arises from many different tissues, most of which are not joints per se, I don't recommend glucosamine and chondroitin for low-back-pain conditions.

Herbal Products and Back Pain

A number of herbal preparations are claimed to bring relief from pain. Unfortunately, there's little clinical evidence to back up these claims. Support for their use comes primarily from folk medicine and from a few animal and test-tube experiments, rather than full-fledged clinical trial research. Herbal remedies are more actively regulated in Germany, where an expert committee found that only three herbs—arnica flower, devil's claw root, and willow bark—have analgesic properties. But arnica is toxic in large doses and cannot be recommended. The other two herbs may relieve pain because they help reduce inflammation.

An important factor to consider when choosing herbal products is that in the United States no governmental body controls the quality or amount of active ingredient in them. Nor is there any guarantee of the purity of these products. Therefore, if you decide to purchase herbal products, buy only products made by reputable companies. Remember: caveat emptor—buyer beware!

Herbal remedies are certainly popular, but how effective are they for back-pain relief? Unfortunately, there's not enough evidence to provide much guidance. Herbal supplements are not subject to the same rigorous testing as medications, which must be approved by the U.S. Food and Drug Administration before they can be marketed in the United States. Complicating matters further, some herbal remedies may interfere with conventional medications you may be taking, especially NSAIDs. Table 7.1 summarizes what is known about three herbs that are often promoted as pain relievers. Given the uncertainties and drug interactions, I

Table 7.1

Herbs and Back-Pain Relief: A Far-from-Clear Picture

Herb (Formulation)	Claims and Evidence	
Devil's claw root (capsules, tea, tincture, oral preparations)	A few studies suggest that devil's claw may improve pain and mobility in people with osteoarthritis, lessening the need for pain medication. Studies on its effectiveness in treating low-back pain have been contradictory.	
Feverfew (capsules, powdered, or chopped dried leaves)	Some studies have found that fever-few may reduce the frequency and severity of migraine headaches.	
Willow bark (tablets)	There have been few controlled studies of willow bark in humans. However, because a compound in aspirin is also found in willow bark, scientists understand how willow bark works. Some clinical studies have found that willow bark can help ease back pain and pain from osteoarthritis.	

NOTE: Children and women who are pregnant or breast-feeding should not use any of these herbs because there is either too little information about them or they have been found to be harmful in these populations.

Side Effects and Interactions	Comments
Devil's claw is generally well tolerated, but side effects may include headache, ringing in the ears, loss of taste and appetite, and diarrhea. This herb may interact with a number of drugs, including anticoagulants, antiplatelet drugs, and medicines for heart conditions, stomach acidity, pain, inflammation, cholesterol, and gout. It may also react with ginkgo biloba, garlic, and the herb bitter melon. If you are using one of these drugs or herbal products, check with your doctor before using devil's claw.	People with ulcers should not take devil's claw. People with the following conditions should consult their doctors before using this herb: diabetes, heart conditions, and gallstones. People undergoing surgery should also talk to their doctors before taking devil's claw. It is not known whether use of devil's claw for longer than three to four months is safe or effective.
Feverfew is generally well tolerated; the most common side effects are mouth inflammation or ulcers, and loss of taste. Feverfew may increase the chance of bleeding if taken with anticoagulants (blood thinners) or antiplatelet drugs, ginkgo biloba, garlic, or anti-inflammatory pain relievers, such as aspirin. Feverfew may also increase the effectiveness of some pain relievers. Some animal studies indicate that feverfew could worsen symptoms of depression or reduce the effectiveness of certain antidepressants. If you have a history of depression or are using an antidepressant, talk to your doctor before taking this herb.	Anyone allergic to the following should avoid feverfew: chrysanthemums, daisies, marigolds, or any member of the *Compositae* plant family, including ragweed. Potential withdrawal symptoms if use of herb is stopped suddenly include rebound headaches, anxiety, sleep disturbances, and muscle stiffness or pain.
Side effects are the same as those for aspirin: gastrointestinal bleeding, nausea, and vomiting. Willow bark should not be taken with aspirin or NSAIDs.	People allergic to aspirin or NSAIDs and children with a fever should not take willow bark.

don't recommend them for back pain. If you are considering using them, talk with your doctor first.

A Prudent Approach

Complementary therapy is a big field with lots of choices. If nothing else, come away from this chapter with two concepts: One, always thoroughly check out the therapy and its practitioner before embarking on a course of treatment. Two, always ask your doctor for his or her opinion. Your hurting back is too vulnerable to risk making a mistake.

Part IV

Managing Your Back Condition

Chapter 8

Nonsurgical Treatments for Your Backache

We've discussed how the back works and the many conditions that can give rise to back pain, as well as the frequent difficulty in diagnosing the specific cause of it. And we've addressed pain management—the first step in treating any back problem. Now we move on to other types of treatments. Let's first talk about nonsurgical treatments, including the important role of rehabilitative exercise—in particular, stretching, strengthening, and aerobic conditioning.

But before we delve into treatment details, let me give you the big picture, and today's medical consensus, on the most appropriate approach to treating back pain. The vast majority of cases of acute back pain are due to nonspecific sprain and strain and will clear up without medical intervention within thirty days or so. With regard to medical intervention, it's hard to compete against such a favorable prognosis. Fancy tests and treatments are simply not necessary for garden-variety back pain. All you need do is make yourself comfortable and strive to resume your normal activities as soon as you can. This translates into self-medication, typically with over-the-counter medicines, little or no bed rest, and holding off on rehabilitative back exercises until your severe discomfort has been brought under control. While exercise is generally not appropriate in the early days of an acute back-pain episode, a well-designed exercise program does play an important role a little later, when you can tolerate movement reasonably well. The goal of exercise is not to make your current acute episode go away—it will on its own—but to prevent recurrences. An appropriate exercise program, tailored to the needs of the individual patient, is also important in the treatment of chronic back pain.

Today's consensus of minimum early intervention is based on research conducted over the past fifteen or so years, culminating in an influential review study authored by Drs. Richard Deyo and James Weinstein in the *New England Journal of Medicine* in 2001. (This is one of the seminal studies I mentioned in Chapter 1.) This wait-and-watch approach doesn't apply if your back pain is due to cauda equina syndrome, infection, or another of the "red flag" scenarios described in earlier chapters. These conditions, of course, require immediate medical intervention.

Your Back's Capacity to Heal Itself

If you think back to my description in the Preface of the incapacitating back treatment plan my doctors recommended when I was a graduating medical student, you might wonder how today's 180-degree turn with regard to treatment has come about. It took many years and numerous studies, but back-pain doctors now appreciate that they can trust the remarkable natural healing capacity of the human back. For much of this book I've pointed out the many things that can go wrong with your back. Now it's time to switch horses and talk about how wonderfully the back takes care of itself and how science has been able to document this amazing healing potential we all possess. The truth is that if patients and doctors did nothing, most back problems attributable to sprain-and-strain syndrome and to some pinched nerve syndromes (sciatica) would clear up on their own within a matter of weeks or months. The exception is a compressed nerve syndrome resulting from spinal stenosis, which typically does not have such a rosy prognosis (see Table 8.1). (Less is known about the natural histories of neck syndromes, though they are probably similar.)

The natural healing capacity of your back means that even if your back pain seems unbearable at the onset of an acute episode of sprain-and-strain syndrome, be reassured when your doctor tells you to go home and wait for your back to heal itself—the advice is cutting-edge! Your doctor is confirming you have a back-pain syndrome with a self-limiting natural history. Surgery should not be considered a first step for low-back pain unless you have a "red flag" emergency condition. (I talk about when you might consider surgery in Chapter 9.)

In this chapter, I'll be focusing on two nonsurgical treatment strategies. First, I'll suggest ways for you to make yourself reasonably comfortable while you "wait it out." Second, I'll explain the role of rehabilitative exercise in your recovery and provide exercise suggestions for you to discuss with your medical team.

Waiting Out Acute Back Pain

Waiting it out doesn't mean you coddle yourself and do nothing for weeks on end. Far from it! At the onset of acute back pain, you have three goals, which are to:

- Relieve pain
- Reduce the risk of reinjuring yourself
- Restore function

Table 8.1

Natural Histories of Back-Pain Syndromes When the Back Heals Itself with No Treatment

Syndrome	Within 1–3 Months
Sprain-and-strain	90% of patients recover; 1% will develop chronic pain
Herniated disk (sciatica)	60–80% of patients recover
Lumbar spinal stenosis	Less than 10% of patients recover

Percentages are based on data gathered from patients with low-back pain.

In its early days, acute back pain is typically quite painful, so finding ways to be as pain free as possible is a priority. The nonprescription analgesic (acetaminophen) and anti-inflammatory medications (aspirin, Advil, Motrin, Aleve, and so on) you have in your medicine cabinet at home, and which I talked about in detail in Chapter 6, should be all you need to be reasonably comfortable. If not, or if you find yourself exceeding the recommended daily dose, ask your doctor for something stronger or for a prescription muscle relaxant if you're having severe muscle spasms.

As well as pain-control medication, applying cold and heat, and finding healthy ways to rest your back can contribute to pain relief and injury prevention.

Cold and Heat: Those Good Old Home Remedies

Some techniques in medicine are age-old, for example, the application of superficial cold and heat to treat musculoskeletal pain.

Within 6–12 Months	Comments
80% will have a return of symptoms within a year	After the initial episode, preventing repeat episodes should be a priority.
90% improve by 6 months and 50% are symptom free at one year	1–2% of Americans opt for surgery.
20% of patients will improve in a year; 20% will deteriorate in a year	Surgery may help some patients in the short term, but it is not a cure-all. A 10-year follow-up study at Brigham and Women's Hospital, a Harvard-affiliated hospital, showed that 10 years after surgery 30% of patients had severe pain and 23% had undergone a second operation.

But for all the ubiquitous use of cold and heat to treat both cervical and lumbar pain, there's little conclusive scientific evidence to prove or disprove their long-term benefits. On the other hand, cold and heat do seem to work for some patients. Heat in particular has been shown to provide short-term pain relief for some patients while also reducing their disability. Whatever benefit cold or heat affords, it happens in the early days of an episode. If applications of cold and heat help you, and I have many patients who say the remedies do help them, here are suggestions about how to use them.

It's usual to start with cold, which numbs pain and reduces swelling by constricting blood vessels and dampening the body's inflammatory reaction. You can apply cold to an injured area of the neck or low back by wrapping an ice pack (a bag of frozen peas will do just fine) in a cloth and applying the pack for fifteen to twenty minutes out of every hour. To prevent frostbite, don't apply ice *directly* to the skin for more than a minute.

Heat is believed to reduce pain and stiffness (a feeling of tight-ness and rigidity in the muscles) and relieve muscle spasms. Heat improves the supply of oxygen the blood carries to the back by dilating (enlarging) the blood vessels. You can apply a heat pack directly to a sore or tense area of your back. While you can pur-chase hot packs and moist/dry heating pads, a homemade hot pack works just as well. Heat a damp folded towel in a microwave oven for about ten to sixty seconds, depending on the oven and the towel's thickness. A warm shower or bath will also relax mus-cles and ease joints—especially beneficial before exercising. Tip: You can also do certain back exercises in the shower. If you do, make sure you have a reliable grab rail in the shower or a bona fide shower stool you can sit on.

After the onset of your back injury, wait a day or two for swell-ing to go down before using heat. Use ice for a maximum of fifteen to twenty minutes an hour for the first twenty-four to forty-eight hours. After that, you can alternate ice and heat or use either ice or heat alone, depending on what works best for you. Here's another tip about using cold and heat in conjunction with a rehabilitative exercise program: ice increases stiffness, so you may find it benefi-cial to use heat before stretching and other exercise, followed by an ice pack afterward to minimize swelling. In other words, warm up and cool down.

Bed Rest

Unless you've sustained a significant injury, such as a fracture, prolonged bed rest is not recommended for neck or low-back pain. Occasionally people have such severe pain or spasms when they are upright that initially lying down is the only way to get relief. If this should happen, keep bed rest to a maximum of two days. After a couple of days there's no advantage to staying in bed addi-tional days. More bed rest doesn't equate with a speedier recovery. In fact the opposite is true. Research has shown that people who had two days of bed rest returned to work more quickly than those who were in bed for a week. Moreover, the disadvantages of extended bed rest are considerable. Muscles rapidly decondition, bones thin out, and the risk of blood clots in the legs and pelvis increases.

Other Ways to Rest

Although bed rest should be used sparingly, other types of rest are important aspects of back-pain treatment. This is common sense, but it's worth repeating: avoid quick movements, positions that hurt, or the activity you think provoked the pain. Specific rest techniques can also contribute to reducing pain and preventing further damage to injured structures. So take regular rests, making sure your neck or back is in a healthy position.

Resting Your Neck. Lying down for twenty to thirty minutes gives your neck a break from supporting the considerable weight of your head. Lie on your back, using a pillow under your knees to help your back relax. Support the curve of your neck from the base upward by using a rolled-up towel, foam cylinder, or cervical pillow specially designed to support the neck.

To help rest your neck muscles and protect damaged tissues from painful movements, your doctor may prescribe a cervical collar, made of foam or plastic and fastened with Velcro, to hold your neck upright. If your doctor prescribes such a collar, wear it as needed for a week or so following your injury, removing it several times a day to exercise your neck. Wear it in bed if it helps you sleep. But as soon as you are able, reduce your use of the collar until you can eliminate it entirely. Prolonged or constant use of such collars isn't advisable because it limits range of motion and may cause neck muscles to weaken.

90/90 Rest Position

Lie on your back on the floor with your arms straight by your side. Place a pillow under your head and neck. Bend your hips and knees at 90 degree angles, resting your lower legs on a stool. Breathe gently.

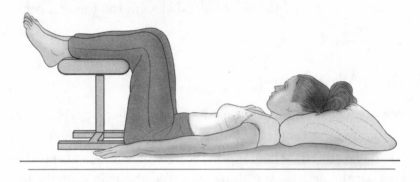

Resting Your Lower Back. The goal is to reduce the forces that standing or sitting impose on your back—especially on the disks, muscles, and ligaments. When you lie on your back, try placing a pillow under your knees. When lying on one side, put pillows under your head and between your knees; when lying on your stomach, put pillows crosswise under your hips. The 90/90 rest position is typically a comfortable position.

Check Out Your Bed. Make sure your mattress is sufficiently firm to support your body because that will help keep your spine in alignment. If you have a sagging bed or mattress, consider investing in an upgrade. Think how many hours you spend asleep and how that translates into healing time for your back.

Getting Going Again

Once your pain is under control and you have a sense of where the trouble spot is in your back, as well as an understanding of what

Catching Back-Pain-Free ZZZs

Getting a good night's sleep is important for many reasons, not just physical. When you have back pain, though, an uninterrupted night's sleep is especially important because sleep provides the perfect opportunity for your spine to rest and recuperate. A hard bed or firm mattress that supports your body alleviates stress on your spine. But is there a perfect sleep position if your back bothers you? Many people find that lying on their sides in the fetal position with knees bent is very comfortable. It relaxes the spine and opens up the spinal canal. If you prefer sleeping on your back, try slipping a pillow under your knees. Ultimately, the best position for you is the one that affords you the most comfortable night's sleep.

you can and can't do without causing yourself a lot of discomfort, it's time to think about getting going again. In medical parlance, it's time to restore functionality. The most effective way of doing this is by embarking upon a graduated rehabilitative exercise program. This involves determining which type of exercises would help your type of back problem and which would fit in with your lifestyle. This latter is "doctor speak" for saying deciding on which exercises to work on is one thing; being motivated to make the time to regularly exercise is something else.

Unless people were highly motivated to exercise regularly before the onset of their back problem, many back-pain sufferers find that consistent follow-through with an exercise program can be the hardest part of a treatment regimen. As a typical sprain-and-strain patient myself, I can speak from experience about the degree of resolve needed to stick with an exercise program! You can have all the best intentions but still find staying with (or starting) a rehabilitative workout a challenge. The carrot to dangle before yourself is the knowledge that research has proven that combining a rehabilitative exercise program with other treatments for your back problem will help your back—and neck—heal faster and enable you to resume your normal activities sooner. After whiplash injury, for example, people are less likely to develop chronic pain, and they heal faster, if they start gentle exercise as soon as possible. Similarly, the value of starting rehabilitative exercise early for low-back pain has been documented many times in the scientific literature.

The benefits of exercise are far-reaching. A properly tailored exercise program will not only help you move more comfortably, repair and strengthen damaged tissues, and regain range of motion, but you'll also have more energy, sleep better, and begin to feel happier and more self-confident. Your family, friends, and work colleagues will be delighted and relieved to see you become your "old" self again. And as I've mentioned, if you "stick with the program" after you've recovered, you'll dramatically decrease your risk of a repeat episode. I talk about this preventive aspect of exercise in Chapter 10.

Sign Up with an Exercise Professional

The exercise approach I'm about to discuss falls under the rubric of rehabilitative treatment and as such should be discussed with your back doctor and whoever else is on your treatment team *before* you start exercising. I'm not, therefore, going to design an exercise program for your specific back problem—nor should I. Too risky. I hope by this point in the book I've conveyed the complexity of the workings of your spine and the vulnerability of the nervous system it protects should anything go wrong with your back. Because the stakes are high, it's advisable to get guidance from a professional who will interview and examine you. Exercise is an essential and powerful tool that will help heal your back, but it has the potential to be a double-edged sword. The wrong exercise at the wrong time or even the right exercise done the wrong way can make things worse. Unless your back pain is the result of run-of-the-mill sprain-and-strain syndrome that is likely to clear up in a matter of weeks, I strongly recommend you talk with a doctor, physical therapist, or qualified trainer before you embark on a rehabilitative exercise program. A trained and experienced professional will individualize an exercise program to meet your needs, guide you through appropriate exercise sequences, and motivate you to work hard enough to see results but not so hard that you induce further injury. I direct this advice to all back-pain sufferers, regardless of their exercise habits before the onset of their back problem. People who were in the habit of exercising regularly before they had a back problem need to remember that rehabilitative exercise is not "exercise as usual." You're now much less conditioned than you were prior to the injury, which means there's a substantial risk of reinjury.

Let's look now at the types of exercise beneficial for back disorders, get acquainted with the principles these exercises are based on, and introduce some exercise examples for you to discuss with your professional exercise guide.

Principles of Rehabilitative Exercise for Back Pain

A rehabilitative exercise program for the back aims to strengthen the muscles of the back, abdomen, hips, and buttocks; and also increase flexibility, especially of the hamstrings, the muscles at the back of your thighs. A well-designed program should include three types of exercises in varying degrees depending on the nature of the back problem. There should be exercises that *strengthen* the core muscles I've just described; and that *stretch* and increase flexibility and range of motion (the amount that a joint moves in specified directions). The program should also include low-impact *aerobic* (cardiovascular) exercises that improve endurance and cardiovascular fitness as well as releasing endorphins, the body's natural painkillers. Although some exercises can be categorized according to type, many exercises overlap, incorporating elements of other exercise types. Developing endurance, for example, can often be built into an exercise by simply increasing the length of time you perform that exercise. Many experts recommend an increase in exercise intensity of 10–15 percent per week. Applied to cycling, this would mean ten minutes daily in week one; eleven to twelve minutes daily in week two; and thirteen to fourteen minutes daily in week three. This may sound like slow progress, but it's generally safe and your daily bike time would double in two months. But again, I want to stress that putting together a program that will help and not hurt you, and that may change over time, requires professional guidance.

How Far Should You Be Able to Reach?

Your neck is the most flexible portion of your spine. If you have a full range of motion, you should be able to:

- Touch your chin nearly to your chest
- Look almost straight up to the sky

What Is Range of Motion?

Range of motion refers to the amount that a joint moves in specified directions. For example, the knee can generally move from being essentially straight (zero degrees of flexion) to being bent 120 degrees. We all recognize when we have limited range of motion. Some of this limitation can be the product of advancing years because range of motion decreases somewhat with age. Over time, your ability to flex and extend your neck, bend or rotate your head from side to side, bend your back forward and backward, and twist and turn your spine may diminish. Limited range of motion is influenced by joint destruction due to arthritis and stiff muscles. The hamstring muscles at the back of your thighs, for example, are notorious for stiffening up and making it hard to bend forward and touch your toes with your hands.

- Rotate your head until the point of your chin is over your shoulders
- Bend your head halfway to your shoulder

Although less flexible than your neck, your lower back should allow you to do the following with your knees straight:

- Bend forward to touch your ankles, or just above your ankles
- Arch backward with some difficulty
- Twist and turn to look behind you

Moving your neck and back through their complete range of motion daily can help prevent pain and maintain motion.

Flexion and Extension Stretches

Back exercises can also be characterized as *flexion* (bending forward) or *extension* (bending backward) exercises. As you bend forward, you widen the spaces between the vertebrae, reducing pressure on the nerves. Flexion exercises for the low back stretch back and hip muscles and strengthen abdominal and buttock muscles. Flexion exercises, though, can exacerbate a pinched nerve syndrome, such as herniated disk, so check with your doctor first. Extension exercises, which are believed to open up the spinal canal and develop muscles that support the spine, can help people with herniated disks by reducing pressure on the nerve root. Extension exercises, though, aren't appropriate for people with spinal stenosis, for whom bending forward is much more comfortable.

Guidelines for Exercising

The back is meant to move; indeed, lack of movement is bad for the back. Remember to respect the power of exercise. When exercising on your own, follow these safety guidelines:

- Always warm up before you start exercising. Take a warm shower, apply a warm pad, or engage in a gentle aerobic activity, such as walking or riding an exercise bike.
- Perform exercises slowly and carefully.
- Include a balanced mix of exercises in each session: flexion and extension exercises; exercises for the right and left side of the body. Yoga practitioners will be familiar with this concept.
- Remember to breathe. Paying attention to your breathing will help you focus on the exercise. Stretching as you breathe out (exhale) will help you relax your muscles and gently extend the stretch with less risk of injury. (This is another concept yoga practitioners will recognize.)

What Goes Forward Should Go Backward

If your back condition permits, try and balance forward bends with a backward stretch. Known as a standing lumbar extension, this is a simple exercise to do if you have been in a flexed position for some time.

Standing Lumbar Extension

Stand with your feet slightly apart and your hands on the top of your buttocks. While looking up, push your hips forward slightly and gently bend backward. Keep your knees straight. Hold for 10 seconds. Relax. Repeat 10 times.

- Apply ice after a workout as needed, especially when you first begin, to minimize swelling and discomfort.
- Hurting for a short while after exercising is to be expected and shouldn't prevent you from exercising. But use your judgment. Never exercise to a point that causes pain. If an exercise is causing moderate or severe pain, stop, apply ice, and don't repeat the exercise until you consult a health

professional. You may be doing the wrong exercise for your
condition.

* Stop exercising if you become light-headed.

Strengthening and Stretching the Muscles of Your Back

In Chapter 3, we explained the importance of the relationship of
muscles, ligaments, and tendons to a healthy, functioning back. You
don't need to become a champion weight lifter, but to relieve and
prevent neck and low-back pain, the muscle groups in your neck and
lower back need to be strong enough to maintain proper posture as
you sit, walk, bend, and do the specialized activities you engage in
during your work and recreational life. Exercises that develop muscle strength are categorized as isometric and isotonic. With isometric exercise, the muscle does not change length as it contracts; with
isotonic exercise, muscles move against a fixed resistance. Here are
examples of isometric and isotonic exercises to show you how the
principles can work to strengthen the muscles of the neck.

Isometric Neck Strengtheners

Isometrics are muscle-building exercises in which you contract
your muscles against resistance (a weight or a wall) but there is no
movement. A good example is putting your palms together and
pressing. For instance, to strengthen your rotation muscles, place
your right hand on the right side of your head. Try to rotate your
head to the right, resisting with your hand, for a count of ten;
and then repeat on the left. In the three exercises described here,
as with the one for your rotation muscles, you use your hands to
provide resistance as you exercise your neck muscles without mov-

Isometric Strengtheners

A. Anterior neck muscles

This exercise can also be done in a sitting position—at the office, for example; or lying down with your knees bent and feet flat on the floor. Place your palm on your forehead and press gently as you try to bring your chin to your chest. Your neck muscles will tighten without your head moving. Hold for a count of 10.

B. Posterior neck muscles

Place one or both hands behind your head and use them as resistance as you press your head backward. Hold for a count of 10.

C. Side neck muscles

Place your right palm on the right side of your head, using it as resistance as you try to bend your right ear toward your shoulder. Hold for a count of 10. Repeat on the left.

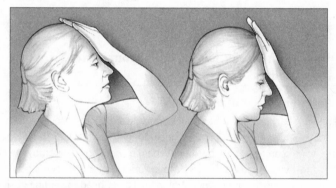

A. Anterior

B. Posterior

C. Side

ing them. Work against the resistance for up to ten seconds at a time, then ease off the pressure and relax. Isometric exercises are often emphasized early in rehabilitation because muscle use is controlled and the risk of injury is low.

Isotonic Neck Strengtheners

Isotonic exercises, such as lifting free weights, require that your muscles move against a resistance (weight) to build strength and improve joint mobility. In the isotonic neck exercises shown here, the weight of your head provides the resistance. Make your motions smooth and controlled, taking about four seconds for each repetition. Work up to three sets of twenty repetitions. Once you can

Isotonic Neck Strengthening Using Your Head as the Weight

A. Anterior neck muscles

Lie on your back with your head supported on a neck roll. Move your chin toward your lower neck, lifting your head but not your neck or shoulders. Lower your head to starting position. Variation (not shown): Remove neck roll and rest your head on the bed. Move your chin toward your chest, lifting your head and neck but not your shoulders. Lower head to starting position and relax.

B. Posterior neck muscles

Lie on your stomach with your head just off the edge of a bed (but not hanging). Raise your head upward a few inches; then relax to starting position.

C. Side neck muscles

Lie on your left side. Looking straight ahead, lift your head to move your right ear toward your right shoulder. Return to starting position and relax. Repeat lying on your right side.

repeat these exercises easily, a physical therapist or trainer can show you how to increase the resistance with the use of special exercise equipment, rubber resistance bands, or weights.

Stretches for Your Neck

Studies have suggested that exercises to strengthen neck muscles may be more effective compared with other types of activity such as stretching and aerobics. But depending on the nature of your neck pain or injury, your physical therapist or professional exercise guide may suggest neck stretches such as the Side-to-Side Stretch, in which you bend your right ear toward your right shoulder, keeping your gaze forward and your shoulders down and relaxed. (If

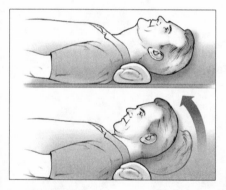

A. Anterior

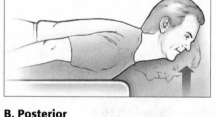

B. Posterior

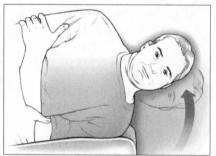

C. Side

you want, you may place your right hand on your head and gently pull to encourage greater bend.) Place your left hand on your left shoulder to keep it down as you stretch. Hold your stretch for about ten seconds; then repeat on the left side. Other similar neck stretches are shown here. (If you find the Chin Retraction exercise to be painful, try it lying down on your back. Tuck your chin in and push the back of your head into the pillow. Hold for a second or two and release. Your head never leaves the pillow. If pain

Neck Stretches

A. Forward stretch

Starting from a neutral position, stretch your neck downward with your chin toward your chest. Hold for 10 seconds. Slowly tilt your head one inch to the right, and to the left.

A. Forward

B. Backward stretch

Next, extend your neck backward to look at the ceiling. Hold for 10 seconds, then slowly tilt your head one inch to the right and one to the left. As you do this, you may find you can extend your neck farther back.

B. Backward

increases or you develop numbness or tingling, stop and contact your doctor.)

Head Rolls. Drop your head to your chest with your arms relaxed at your side. Gently roll your head from left to right several times, passing through the dropped center position each time. You can build up to a complete circular roll of the head, which includes a roll to the back. Caution: If you have a pinched nerve syn-

Chin Retraction (Neck Muscles)

A.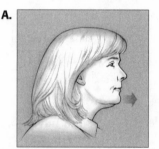

A. Sit in a neutral position looking straight ahead. Allow your head to protrude slightly forward into a normal resting position.

B.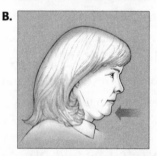

B. Next, slowly glide your head backward, tucking your chin in until you have pulled your head and chin as far back as they will go. Keep your head level and don't tilt or nod your head. Move slowly back and forth between the two positions 10 times.

C.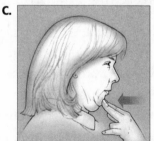

C. For a stronger stretch, gently apply pressure to your chin with your fingers and release. Repeat every two hours as needed.

drome, you should not do this exercise without first consulting a professional.

Stretching and Strengthening Your Shoulders

Tense or weak shoulder muscles contribute significantly to neck pain. Here are a couple of stretching and strengthening shoulder exercises you might try.

Shoulder Rolls. Looking ahead with your head positioned comfortably at the top of your spine, and with your arms relaxed at your side, gently roll each shoulder in a circular movement backward several times and then forward several times. Repeat with the other shoulder. Repeat with both shoulders. Make sure your head doesn't poke forward out of alignment with your spine as you do the rolls; and never force the roll.

Shoulder Shrug. Stand with your arms at your sides. For a minute or two, slowly and rhythmically lift your shoulders up and back, then relax them back down. This exercise can be done holding weights in your hands (start with a one- or two-pound weight and build up to ten pounds).

Stretching and Strengthening Your Lower Back

Here is a representative selection of exercises that are beneficial for various types of back-pain problems. My selection is not exhaustive; there are many more. Nor is my selection intended to be an off-the-shelf exercise program you can follow without guidance. My hope is to provide you with exercise ideas you can discuss with your physical therapist or physician.

Posterior Pelvic Tilt

Strengthens the muscles of the abdomen and buttocks. Lie on your back with your knees bent, feet on the floor, and arms by your side. Attempt to flatten your lumbar spine and get it as close to the floor as possible. Hold the position for 5–10 seconds and release. This exercise can be repeated many times.

Curl Up

Strengthens the muscles of the abdomen. Lie on your back on a mat. Put your hands beneath the small of your back and bend both knees to help stabilize your spine. While contracting your abdominal wall muscles so your navel is pulled toward your spine, raise your head and shoulders a few inches off the floor. Pause and hold that position for 10–20 seconds. Don't forget to breathe! Lower your head and shoulders. Do 8–12 repetitions. Rest and repeat the set.

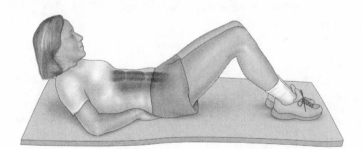

Elbow Prop

Stretches the muscles of the back. Lie on the floor or another flat surface. Keep your legs and pelvis against the flat surface, elbows bent and close to your body, and lower arms and hands against the flat surface. This is the same position as the standing lumbar extension I described earlier, only rather than standing, now the body is supported by the flat surface. Hold the position for 30–60 seconds. Relax and repeat. For increased extension, push up the top half of the body by using the arms until the elbows are straight.

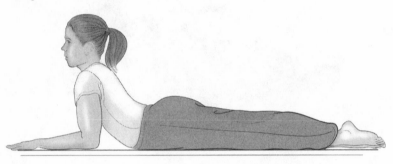

Trunk Extension

Stretches the muscles of the low back and buttocks, and upper back and neck. Lie on your stomach on a mat with your face up off the floor. Your arms should stretch out in front of you. Now raise your arms and legs as high as possible while extending your trunk. Hold for a count of 6–10 while breathing normally. Release slowly. Do 5–8 repetitions. Rest and repeat the set. Variation: Raise just your right leg and opposite (left) arm during the first set; just your left leg and right arm during the second set; and both arms and legs during the third set.

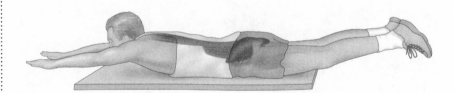

Lower-Back Stretch and Hip Stretch

Stretches the low-back muscles. Lie flat on your back with both legs
extended. Keep your neck on the floor, but look down toward your chest.
Bend both knees and clasp them with your hands, pulling your knees
gently toward your shoulders as far as they will comfortably go. Breathe in
deeply and exhale, bringing the knees closer as you breathe out. You'll feel
compression in your hips and a stretch in your lower back. Hold for 20–30
seconds while breathing normally. Variation: Pull one knee toward you while
keeping the other knee bent. Alternate knees.

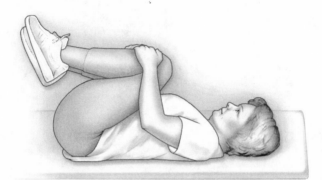

Cat Stretch

Stretches the muscles of the back and shoulders. Rest on your knees, then
lower your head and reach forward along the floor with one arm, then both
arms. Hold for 20–30 seconds. Relax, then repeat.

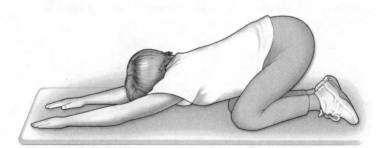

Bridge

Stretches the muscles of the back, buttocks, and hamstrings. Lie on your back on a mat with your knees bent and your feet flat on the floor. Put your hands next to your hips with palms flat on the floor. Keep your back straight as you lift your buttocks as high as you can off the mat, using your hands for balance only. Pause. Lower your buttocks without touching the mat, then lift again. Do 8–12 repetitions. Rest and repeat the set. This exercise may be difficult; don't do it if it's painful.

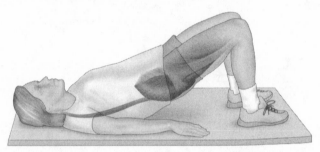

Double Hip Rotation

A gentle twist that stretches the muscles of the hip, side, and, to a lesser extent, neck. Lie on your back with your knees bent and feet flat on the floor. Keep your shoulders on the floor at all times. Gently lower both legs to one side, keeping your knees together, and turn your head to the opposite side. Hold for 20–30 seconds. Bring your knees back to center and repeat on the other side.

   Caution: While this exercise is beneficial for some people, it's essentially a twist and you shouldn't do the exercise without first talking with your medical team. If you have had a hip replacement, you should certainly check with your doctor before attempting this exercise.

Stretching Your Hamstrings

The muscles at the back of your thighs can contribute to low-back pain. We know that people with low-back pain tend to have tight hamstrings, and, consequently, exercises that stretch the hamstrings bring back-pain relief. Here are some representative exercises:

- Bend forward from the waist, keep your knees straight, touch your toes, and hold the position for several seconds. Gently uncurl to a standing upright position.
- If that's too painful, sit on a chair with your legs on another chair in front of you. Keeping your legs straight, reach out and touch your toes. You can do this one leg at a time.
- If you can lie comfortably on the floor, lie on your back with your buttocks against the wall and your legs straight up the wall. Try to straighten your knee by pushing into the wall. You can alternate legs.

All hamstring stretches should be done carefully to avoid injury.

Low-Impact Aerobic Exercises for Acute Back Pain

The low-impact aerobic exercises of walking, riding an exercise bike, and water therapy are more suitable for episodes of acute back pain. High-impact exercises—such as running or aerobic dancing—risk injury to your back.

- **Walking.** If possible, walk two to three miles at least three times a week.

- **Biking.** An exercise bike may be less stressful on the back than walking, which itself is gentle on the back.
- **Water therapy.** If your back is very painful or if you're elderly, doing exercises in water is especially beneficial because water supports the body, which takes pressure off the spine while you exercise.

For most people, the natural healing properties of the back, aided by home remedies and an appropriately designed, graduated rehabilitative exercise program, will take care of most back problems. But for those few who are not helped by these approaches or who can't wait out the natural healing process, surgery is an option, which we discuss in Chapter 9.

Chapter 9

Is Surgery Right for You?

Considering the large number of people who have back problems, relatively few people have back surgery. But here's an interesting statistic: the rate of back surgery is five times higher in the United States than it is in England and Scotland. All this additional surgery doesn't seem to be helping Americans, however. The rate of work disability is just as high in the United States as it is in these other countries. Is too much back surgery done in the United States? Too little in the United Kingdom? We can't say for sure. But these widely differing rates of surgery do tell us that physicians and their patients are making different decisions about how to care for back pain in these different parts of the world. In this chapter we're going to look closely at how these decisions—whether to have surgery or not—are made.

How Do You Decide?

For the most part, back surgery is *elective*, meaning the decision to operate is made by the patient, in consultation with his or her doctor. The exception is when back pain signifies a "red flag" situation such as cauda equina syndrome, an infection of the spine, tumor, or traumatic injury that has caused severe damage to the vertebrae and spinal cord. In these *emergency* situations, the spine surgeon will make most of the decisions. But for other situations, you're in the driver's seat. When is surgery right for you? There's no "right" answer; only your answer. How then do you decide?

A number of factors will influence your decision. The first is whether your back problem can be helped by surgery. Not all can. In fact, the vast majority of neck and lower-back problems can't be improved by surgical procedures. In general, surgery is useful if you have symptoms arising from compression of the spinal nerve roots. Your doctor will let you know whether indeed you are a surgical candidate. Doctors can disagree on this important point, so sometimes a second opinion can be helpful.

A Tale of Two Patients

I introduced you to Ellen in Chapter 5. When I met her, Ellen was suffering from exceedingly painful sciatic symptoms due to a compressed nerve in her low back. This diagnosis was confirmed by MRI. An active woman, Ellen wanted relief quickly but didn't want to risk the complications of surgery. After reviewing her options, she chose epidural injections over surgery, followed by a graduated exercise program with a physical therapist. She had a couple of minor setbacks the next year, which responded to NSAIDs and patience. Eight years later, Ellen remains active and continues to exercise.

Sam is a self-employed business consultant whose work necessitates flying to meet with clients. Being self-employed, Sam is more flexible than many people. He is able to schedule his business appointments and make time for his exercise program. An avid tennis player whom I met ten years ago when he was in his forties, Sam has had the misfortune to develop sciatica and cervical radiculopathy at an early age—in his thirties. In the intervening years, he has continued to be plagued with compressed nerve syndromes in his lumbar and cervical spine and now has also developed spinal stenosis. As a patient with early and aggressive disk degeneration, Sam's view was that epidural injections, which admittedly helped, provided only temporary pain relief. Sam opted for surgery—not once but twice. He's had laminectomy—a procedure I describe later in this chapter—to decompress a nerve root in his lumbar spine and a similar surgery to decompress a nerve root in his cervical spine. Each time he recovered quickly and resumed his busy lifestyle.

Ellen decided against surgery; Sam felt it was the best option for him. They both continue to exercise and lead active lives. Two patients; two different solutions.

Let's say you're suffering from a pinched nerve syndrome, such as a herniated disk or spinal stenosis, and less invasive methods haven't provided sufficient relief. Surgery could help. What do you need to consider? One important consideration is whether the condition will get better on its own. Herniated disk syndromes very often get better over time. Spinal stenosis, on the other hand, is not as likely to improve.

But it's not that cut-and-dried. If you have a herniated disk syndrome, you may not have the time—or the personality—to wait out the back's natural healing cycle. People with very demanding jobs, home responsibilities, and other pursuits may elect surgery early in the course to get back to their busy lifestyles quicker. That's perfectly reasonable. On the other hand, someone with relatively few demands at work and home may be willing to wait out the natural healing cycle. Also reasonable; the choice is yours. How you view surgery is another factor. I've had patients with comparable back conditions who considered all these factors and made different decisions.

Do You Meet Surgical Criteria?

Before considering surgery, ask yourself if you meet the following criteria:

- Have you been in substantial distress for a sufficient period—usually a minimum of six weeks—to convince both you and your doctor that the more conservative approaches described thus far in this book won't provide sufficient relief?
- Is there clear evidence that the source of your pain can be addressed by surgery? Since most spine surgeries involve decompressing nerve roots, the critical question is whether the symptoms arise from nerve root compression.
- Has a reliable imaging procedure, such as a CT scan or MRI, shown that a surgically correctable anatomical abnormality is putting pressure on a nerve root? If diagnostic tests don't reveal clear signs of spinal nerve root compression, the origin of the low-back pain may lie elsewhere in the body.

Weighing Surgical Risks and Benefits

All back operations involve a degree of risk: infection at the site of the incision, nerve damage, bleeding due to damage to large vessels that lie in front of disks, heart attack, blood clots in the lungs or legs, pneumonia, and failure to regain consciousness (extremely rare). On average, one of these serious conditions can happen about one time in a hundred. You can minimize the risk of these complications by selecting an orthopedist or neurosurgeon who was trained and has experience in spine surgery, is board certified for orthopedic or neurosurgery, and has done a large number of these operations.

To find a surgeon ask your primary care doctor for a referral and get recommendations from family and friends who've recently undergone successful back surgery. The surgeon you choose should be concerned about you and answer your questions. You also need to ask the surgeon about his or her experience and comfort level with your specific operation. Your surgeon should answer all your questions directly and candidly.

Another important risk of surgery is that it might not help you. Up to 10 percent of patients who have spine surgery for herniated disks or spinal stenosis go on to have another surgery within a few years because the first one did not work. This statistic underscores the importance of making sure that you meet the criteria for surgery we discussed earlier.

Questions for You to Answer

Do you have a doctor you can ask questions of and discuss concerns with? A careful and thorough discussion between you and your doctor will help you reach an informed decision that reflects your own values and preferences. Here are the kinds of questions you should ask yourself:

- Do you fully understand everything there is to understand about your back-pain problem? Your answer should include up-to-date information about your condition, the various ways to treat it, and the likely outcomes of these treatments.

- Have the risks and benefits offered by surgery for your back problem been explained to you in a way that you understand?
- Do you know the likely natural history of your back condition so you can make an assessment between a wait-and-watch approach and surgery? (You might want to review the natural history table in Chapter 8.)
- How do you feel about taking risks of any sort? Consider your personality, lifestyle, age, other medical conditions, and so forth.
- How do you feel about the risks associated with both the surgical and the nonsurgical treatment options for your back problem?
- Do you appreciate that surgery doesn't always guarantee success in terms of pain control? Sometimes surgeries are repeated, but the success rate of repeat surgeries is lower than first surgeries.
- How much functionality do you want and how much risk are you willing to take to get it? If you're a professional athlete, you'll want more functionality and be prepared to take more risk. For most people the stakes aren't so high.

Surgery for Disk Disease

More than 90 percent of people with herniated disks will recover within six weeks to several months without surgery. But if you are among the other 10 percent—or if you don't have the time to wait—surgery is something to consider. Several disk surgery options exist, so it's important to work with your surgeon to determine which operation is best for you. One of the most common types of disk surgery performed is a *diskectomy*, the removal of a portion of a damaged disk. (More than 350,000 diskectomies are performed annually in the United States.)

Several types of diskectomies are available. Something worth bearing in mind with regard to all diskectomy procedures, however, is that although they provide better pain relief over a four-year period than nonsurgical treatments, it's not clear whether surgery is more of an advantage after a much longer period of follow-up, such as ten years. And studies of two less invasive types of procedures—percutaneous diskectomy and laser diskectomy—show that these newer techniques do not yet have the same success rate as standard diskectomy.

Standard Diskectomy

Standard diskectomy, which is defined as open back surgery because more of the back is exposed during surgery, involves making an opening in the spinal canal between adjacent laminae (the platelike parts of each vertebra that join in the midline) and removing material protruding from the abnormal disk. Since the problem area is directly exposed during surgery, the risk of inadvertent damage to neighboring bone, ligaments, and nerve roots is minimized, and the surgeon can remove the maximum amount of the protruding disk material. If a significant portion of the disk protrudes into the spinal canal, compressing a nerve root, the surgeon will trim the bulging portion. He or she will also remove some portion of the soft part of the disk between the vertebrae. Sometimes the protruding disk material actually detaches, forming what's called a *free fragment*. The surgeon will remove such free disk fragments during surgery.

Diskectomy often requires a laminectomy. In this procedure, the surgeon cuts out all or part of one or both laminae (the bony plates of each vertebra), so that he or she has better access to a herniated disk. The bulging portions of the disk are removed through this opening. (This is one of several procedures that Sam had.)

The odds that a disk operation will relieve back pain and sciatica depend on a number of factors. If the imaging tests, symptoms, and physical examination all point to the same abnormality (for example, a disk protrusion at L4–5 causing right L5 nerve root compression), then the likelihood of improvement is over 90 percent. This means if patients are carefully chosen to make sure the operation is appropriate, over 90 percent will improve.

After Surgery. A hospital stay of one to several days is typically followed by a course of physical therapy at home. During the first six weeks or so following surgery, try not to sit for longer than fifteen to twenty minutes at a time. When you do sit, recline your chair back about 30 degrees from the vertical. Avoid bending, lifting, and twisting, but start walking as soon as you can tolerate it. Two weeks after the operation, you can begin stationary bicycling and swimming. If you develop back or leg pain, ease off and talk with your doctor. You can usually resume normal, non-vigorous activities six weeks following surgery, although the decision is up to you and your surgeon. You can speed up or slow down the schedule according to your situation.

Microdiskectomy. This is a type of standard diskectomy that involves a smaller incision. Its benefits include a shorter hospital stay and less risk of the postsurgical complications that can go with a longer hospitalization, such as postoperative blood clots. The procedure does have some drawbacks, but its success rate is similar to that of standard diskectomy.

Percutaneous Diskectomy

A less invasive technique than standard diskectomy, this procedure involves the removal of a portion of a damaged disk through an instrument inserted in the back (see Figure 9.1). The surgeon inserts a probe, a hollow tube, through an incision. Visualizing the site by fluoroscopy, in which x-rays project a continuous image of the body's internal structures on a fluorescent screen, the surgeon guides the probe precisely through the skin, muscle sheath, and muscles to reach the affected disk. He or she then guides the probe into the center of the disk and uses an automated cutting-irrigating-suctioning tool, which is inserted through the probe, to remove some of the nucleus and annulus from the herniated disk.

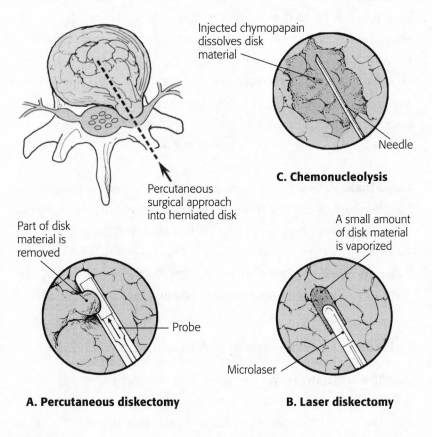

Injected chymopapain dissolves disk material

Needle

C. Chemonucleolysis

Percutaneous surgical approach into herniated disk

Part of disk material is removed

A small amount of disk material is vaporized

Probe

Microlaser

A. Percutaneous diskectomy

B. Laser diskectomy

Figure 9.1

Minimally Invasive Disk Surgery Techniques

Percutaneous diskectomy (A), laser diskectomy (B), and chemonucleolysis (C) all attempt to relieve back pain by removing a portion of the herniated disk.

This delicate operation can reduce both the pressure and volume of the material inside the disk, thus relieving the irritation of the nerve root. The incision is small, the procedure requires local anesthesia only, and you can usually return home the same day or the next. You'll need to avoid sitting for longer than fifteen to twenty minutes at a time, as well as bending, twisting, and lifting for a few weeks.

This procedure, though, has a number of disadvantages when compared to standard diskectomy. Since the compressed nerve root remains hidden from direct observation during the operation, the surgeon often can't be sure that the pressure on it has been reduced or eliminated. Should a bit of the soft center of the disk slip out through the annulus, the surgeon has no way of finding and removing it. Such a free-floating disk fragment can cause pain. In addition, there is a small risk of infection and damage to nerves, organs, and blood vessels in the area.

Laser Diskectomy. This is a variation of percutaneous diskectomy (see Figure 9.1). Rather than removing some of the disk material with a cutting-irrigating-suctioning tool, the surgeon uses a medical laser to vaporize part of the nucleus pulposus. The benefits, risks, and success rates associated with laser diskectomy are the same as those for percutaneous diskectomy.

Intradiscal Electrothermal Annuloplasty (IDET)

Intradiscal electrothermal annuloplasty, which first became available in 1997, is an option for people who have certain kinds of disk problems, such as small herniations, internal disk tears, or mild disk degeneration. In this procedure, a surgeon inserts a hollow needle into the affected disk, threads a thin catheter through the needle, and positions the catheter along the inner wall of the disk. The catheter is then heated, which cauterizes the small nerve fibers in the disk wall in an effort to relieve pain.

Although generally regarded as a safe procedure, IDET is not particularly effective. A 2004 study published in *Spine* found that one year after the procedure, half of those treated were unhappy with the outcome of their therapy; 97 percent continued to have pain, with 29 percent saying they had more pain after IDET than before the procedure. And the percentage of people who were on disability was the same as before treatment.

Chemonucleolysis

Chemonucleolysis was introduced as a less invasive treatment for herniated disks in 1963 but remains controversial. In this technique, an enzyme, chymopapain, is used to dissolve a portion of the herniated disk (see Figure 9.1). While you lie facedown on a table, the surgeon uses x-rays to locate the affected disk and then injects chymopapain into it through a long needle. This causes a chemical reaction that breaks down the nucleus pulposus, releasing water.

The treatment, which is more popular in Europe than it is in the United States, appears to be effective. A 2002 study published in *Neurosurgery*, involving 3,000 people who were treated with chemonucleolysis between 1984 and 1999, found that the success rate was 85 percent. A 2003 Irish study, in which researchers followed 112 people for almost ten years, concluded that chemonucleolysis was a safe and effective treatment when administered to patients who have only one collapsed disk. But this treatment is not for everyone. The best candidates for chemonucleolysis are people who suffer from disk herniation characterized by leg pain and a soft protruded disk rather than a diffuse bulging disk. Younger individuals who have not had their symptoms long and who are able to raise their leg straight in front of them during an exam are considered the best candidates.

Although less invasive than diskectomy, chemonucleolysis can result in several days of severe pain and other unwanted—and occasionally serious—side effects. Risks include severe allergic reactions to the enzyme used in the procedure, ranging from a simple rash, itching, and localized swelling to anaphylactic shock, a life-threatening condition characterized by an extremely rapid, sharp drop in blood pressure. The incidence of such reactions can be significantly reduced, although not eliminated, by the use of a simple skin test for an allergic reaction to the enzyme. Also, if chymopapain should come into contact with certain structures near the disk, it can result in serious neurological damage.

Surgery for Compression (Osteoporotic) Fractures

Vertebral compression fractures due to osteoporosis mainly affect menopausal women. (About one in four menopausal women have suffered a vertebral compression fracture.) The standard treatment was—and still is—to wait it out while the fractured bone heals. This process can take six weeks on average and is very painful. Often opiates are required to provide relief.

In recent years, two new procedures for treating vertebral fractures have grown in popularity: vertebroplasty and kyphoplasty. In many cases, these procedures quickly alleviate pain from spinal fractures, often as soon as the same day! Vertebroplasty and kyphoplasty are suitable to treat only compression fractures, not other types of back-pain problems, and are usually recommended to people who can't tolerate the more conservative measures of rest and pain medications. And while short-term benefits are promising—if not dramatic for some people—more research is needed to determine the long-term benefits and risks associated with the two techniques.

Vertebroplasty

This technique, which was developed in France and first introduced in the United States in 1993, is done on an outpatient basis and takes less than an hour. After you're given mild sedation, the physician inserts a needle into the affected vertebra, using an x-ray for guidance. Bone cement, called *methylmethacrylate*, is then injected into the compressed vertebra, filling the holes and crevices. The cement hardens in about twenty minutes, stabilizing the vertebra, creating a support that helps prevent any further collapse, and alleviating pain.

Serious side effects are uncommon but complications could include infection, bleeding, and leakage of the injected cement causing compression of adjacent nerve tissue. A number of short-term studies have been done on vertebroplasty, and the results indicate that the procedure is safe and for most people significantly reduces pain and helps prevent another collapse. But as yet there are no results from long-term studies. Also, none of the studies have been randomized trials, meaning that it's impossible to determine whether the improvements seen in the patients treated with vertebroplasty might have occurred anyway, without vertebroplasty, as part of the natural healing of the fracture. Vertebroplasty has several technical limitations, including the risk of cement leakage, as I noted above, and an inability to restore the height loss caused by compression fractures.

Kyphoplasty

This procedure is a refinement of vertebroplasty, offering several technical advantages. Like vertebroplasty, kyphoplasty aims to stabilize compressed vertebrae and relieve pain. But it also restores the height of previously compressed vertebrae and reduces spinal deformity.

Kyphoplasty (see Figure 9.2) takes less than an hour, although you may need to remain in the hospital overnight. After you receive mild sedation, a physician inserts a small tubelike instrument into the affected vertebra, using a special viewing instrument called a *fluoroscope* as a guide. Once the instrument is correctly placed, a balloon is inflated, creating a cavity in the bone. The balloon is deflated and removed; then the surgeon injects surgical cement into the cavity. The creation of this cavity minimizes the risk that the cement will leak and pushes the vertebral endplates apart, thus restoring some height. The few studies conducted on kyphoplasty indicate the procedure is safe and provides pain relief. However, as with vertebroplasty, there have been no randomized controlled trials of kyphoplasty, so we can't say for sure whether patients might have improved without the procedure.

Vertebroplasty and Kyphoplasty Cautions. These techniques don't work for everyone, and sometimes pain relief is disappointingly short-lived—for reasons not yet understood. In the absence of long-term studies, concerns about the two techniques remain.

- Will "fixing" one vertebra have a detrimental effect on neighboring vertebrae?
- What, if any, will be the long-term effect of "interfering" with the mechanics of the spine?

What's my bottom line on vertebroplasty and kyphoplasty? When I work with patients who've had a painful compression fracture that is not improving quickly over the first several weeks, I inform them about vertebroplasty and kyphoplasty; help them to understand the risks, drawbacks, and our lack of knowledge about their long-term effects; and compare these with the natural history of compression fracture. Patients can then make up their minds based on an honest appraisal of what we know about these procedures.

 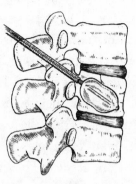

A. Tube insertion   **B. Balloon inflation**

Figure 9.2

Kyphoplasty

This technique restores some height to the treated compressed vertebra. First, a tube is inserted into the vertebra (A). Then a balloon at the end is inflated and deflated, leaving a hollow in the bone (B). Finally, surgical cement is injected into the cavity, shoring up the vertebral endplates.

Surgery for Lumbar Spinal Stenosis

Spinal stenosis is a lot less likely than a herniated disk problem to clear up on its own. This makes surgery attractive. On the other hand, people with spinal stenosis are older and often have other medical and orthopedic conditions. These problems, such as heart and lung disease and osteoarthritis of the hips and knees, increase the risk of complications and can limit their functionality. So patients need to be realistic about the likely results of back surgery.

Lumbar spinal stenosis surgery involves removing the various structures that press on the nerve and contribute to the stenosis. The surgeon makes an incision in the back and removes the lamina, the spinous processes, and (if necessary) portions of the paired facet joints, along with any osteophytes or disk herniation. Sometimes a spinal fusion is performed to fix the position of the vertebrae permanently and prevent future displacement. Rehabilitation variously includes walking, riding a stationary bicycle, or swimming for gradually increasing periods. Between 65 percent to 75 percent of people treated in this way eventually obtain good to excellent results. They find lingering pain can be controlled by non-narcotic or over-the-counter medications; and they can engage in physical activity with few or no restrictions.

Spinal Fusion Surgery

Spinal fusion surgery is used to treat spondylolisthesis, as well as other types of back problems. In this procedure, a surgeon can decompress nerve roots if necessary and fuse adjacent misaligned vertebrae. The success rate for such operations depends on the underlying diagnosis. Fusion is very effective for spondylolisthesis accompanied by spinal stenosis. About 75 percent of patients treated for this condition with spinal fusion improve. However, spinal fusion is also sometimes performed for patients with no evidence of spinal nerve root involvement. In these circumstances, the success of fusion is highly variable. I'm very hesitant about recommending back surgery for patients who do not have symptoms of nerve root compression.

Several different methods of fusion are possible to join two or more adjacent vertebrae. The space between the vertebrae can be bridged with a graft of bone from elsewhere in the body or from a bone bank. The graft also stimulates bone growth in the area of the fusion. In addition, metal screws and plates secured to the vertebrae can be used as internal splints to hold the vertebrae until new bone has consolidated the graft into a strong bony strut. Small cylindrical metal cages may also be inserted into the vertebrae to work as internal splints that hold the vertebrae together while the fusion takes place. These approximately inch-long cages are typically made of titanium.

Following spinal fusion surgery, you may wear a brace, a cast, or neither—depending on the specifics of your operation and the opinion of your surgeon. It usually takes about six months for a spine to fuse.

Successful surgery results in a stable union between the fused vertebrae. Within four to nine months, your body replaces most of the grafted bone at the surgical site with new bone. By reducing motion in the affected area of the spine, a bone fusion relieves the pain caused by abnormal movement. After fusion, your range of spinal motion will be approximately 20 percent to 30 percent less than it was originally. However, compared to your condition before surgery, when pain most likely limited your motion, you're likely to have a greater effective range of movement, as well as freedom from chronic pain. It's very important to be aware that sometimes the fusion can succeed technically—that is, the bones heal together as planned—but the pain doesn't go away. Surgeons can usually get the vertebrae to fuse; the challenge is to offer this procedure to patients whose symptoms will be relieved by the fusion. I make use of second opinions often in this situation.

Bionic Backs: The Advent of Artificial Disks

Artificial hips, limbs, and even artificial heart valves have revolutionized medical care, and this technology is now being applied to the spine. Patients who face the prospect of having spinal fusion now have a new alternative, the implantation of an artificial disk.

In the United States, the FDA approved the first artificial disk for the spine in 2004, but others are in development. Compared to the rigidity of spinal fusion, an artificial disk is designed to mimic a natural disk and provide normal movement between the vertebrae and maintain the disk height between them.

In 1997, a French study reviewed 105 artificial disk placement operations over more than four years and found that 79 percent of those treated had excellent results, with 87 percent of them returning to work. A subsequent ten-year follow-up study of 100 of the original 107 patients by the same researchers, published in 2005, found excellent results, with 91 percent returning to work during the follow-up decade.

There are still a number of unanswered questions about the artificial disk, such as whether introducing foreign material will incite an immunologic reaction that could cause the replacement to fail. I advise patients to seek more than one surgical opinion before undertaking an artificial disk replacement.

Surgery for Other Back Problems

Some other types of back problems that may benefit from prompt surgery include infections, tumors, and certain kinds of fractures. In these situations, timely surgery is essential. Delay may permit the tumor, infection, or other problem to damage the spinal cord or spinal nerve roots.

Infections

Infections can affect the vertebral bone (vertebral osteomyelitis), the epidural space (epidural abscess), or the disk (diskitis). Each of these is a serious infection. If antibiotics are not completely effective, surgery may be necessary. In an operation called a "debridement" or "decompression," the surgeon removes pus and the infected and dead parts of the bone. The surgeon then washes out the affected area with a sterile solution containing antibiotics to kill the bacteria or fungi. A bone fusion is also recommended when large portions of one or more vertebrae must be removed to control the infection. You'll need to take antibiotics for several weeks after surgery.

Tumors

For a bone tumor originating in the spine, surgery may or may not be indicated, depending on a number of factors, including whether the growth is malignant; whether it can be treated by radiation or chemotherapy; whether it's compressing the spinal canal or nerve roots; and whether it's located in a part of the spine where surgical excision is possible. For the operation to cure the disease, the entire cancerous tumor must be removed, along with a portion of healthy bone. When the spine is weakened by the surgical excision of bone or by the destruction of bone by the tumor, the weakened area must be stabilized. This is usually done with metal implants, sometimes supplemented by methylmethacrylate (bone cement) or by bone grafts.

For tumors that have metastasized to the spine from another site—such as the breast or prostate—radiation, surgery, chemotherapy, or some combination of these treatment options is used, as appropriate.

Some tumors, including lipomas, teratomas, ependymomas, and neurofibromas, arise directly from the spinal cord or the nerve roots. Although rare, such growths are often painful. Whether a surgical approach is possible depends on the type of tumor, as well as its size and location.

Dislocations and Vertebral Fractures

Slightly displaced spinal fractures or dislocations usually heal without causing severe pain or spinal instability. Surgery is generally reserved for serious ligament and bone damage. Your doctor will determine the extent of the damage through a physical examination and analysis of imaging studies, such as MRIs.

During an operation, the surgeon can, if necessary, remove bone fragments from the spinal canal and can implant metal plates or rods—either temporarily or permanently—to stabilize the spine and maintain its alignment during healing. Spinal fusion is usually needed to reconstruct or substitute for damaged vertebrae or ligaments, or both.

Knowing When You're Ready to Decide

As I've discussed, there are emergency situations when your doctors will make most of the decisions. For example, the decision of whether to operate in a case of infected epidural abscess will hinge primarily on the judgment of the medical and surgical team and not on your preferences. Fortunately, such emergency situations are very rare and unlikely to confront any of us. Herniated disks, spinal stenosis, and vertebral compression fractures, on the other hand, are common. A decision to have surgery for these conditions is yours to make and you shouldn't make it quickly. Take whatever time you need to explore all your options. Your decision, when you make it, should be self-evident after you've asked all your questions, pored over the information, and thought through who you are and how you wish to live.

After your surgery, you'll most likely be working closely with a physical therapist and your doctor to help you become stronger and facilitate your reentry into an active life. But it doesn't end there. Once you're feeling better, that's when you begin a preventive program to help reduce the number and intensity of any repeat episodes.

Chapter 10

Preventing a Repeat Episode

Avoiding future back problems, particularly those due to sprain-and-strain syndromes, has three components: staying in good physical condition, jettisoning bad lifestyle habits, and practicing back-protective behaviors as you go about your everyday activities.

Stay Fit

Staying active and in good physical condition is the most important thing you can do to maintain a healthy back and protect yourself from a relapse following an initial episode of acute back pain. Being in good physical condition helps prevent back pain by strengthening your back and abdominal muscles.

Physical activity also confers many other benefits. It helps you maintain a healthy weight; improve the efficiency of your heart; reduce your blood pressure and stress level; lower your risk for diabetes and colon cancer; brighten your mood; and keep your mental faculties sharp as you get older. And osteoporosis studies have shown that strength training can slow bone loss and possibly even build bone. It therefore makes sense to exercise regularly, but sensibly. If you've been leading a somewhat sedentary lifestyle, check with your doctor first to make sure you pace yourself appropriately, especially in the beginning.

Start with Low-Impact Exercises

Bicycling (either stationary or regular), swimming, and walking head the list of low-risk, high-benefit activities for most back conditions, as I touched on briefly in Chapter 8. All are low- or minimal-impact exercises that strengthen the erector spinae and abdominal muscles and stimulate secretion of endorphins. None involve awkward or stressful positions that are detrimental to back muscles—for example, forcing them to exert a lot of force. Participating in any or all of these activities at least three times a week is a good strategy for anyone who tends to have recurrent episodes of mild to moderate low-back pain. Since they usually put little burden on your back, these activities offer the benefits of exercise without unduly placing your back at risk. That said, it may be that for your particular condition one or another of these activities consistently makes things worse. Some people find they can't swim the breaststroke because it bothers their backs; others have trouble with bicycling. You shouldn't do exercises that consistently hurt you. I suggest to my patients that they try walking, swimming, and bicycling; you'll probably find each of them comfortable, too. Almost certainly you'll find one or two of them comfortable. Let these become the core of your exercise program.

Use Your Common Sense

Countless other exercises and activities can strengthen your back, as well as your entire body. Choose any one (or any combination) of them that makes sense and feels good—and pursue it regularly.

However, if you're recuperating from a back-pain episode or if you feel the warning twinges of a repeat episode waiting in the wings, cut back on your activities. Also, the motions and positions used in some sports pose a threat to your back and can thus offset any potential benefit of exercise. Football, gymnastics, wrestling, weight lifting, rowing (crew), and ballet, for instance, involve a relatively high risk for back injury because of the extension, twisting, lifting, or impacts involved. Other unnatural motions that could induce pain include back arching (during gymnastics and diving); twisting (while hitting a golf ball, swinging at a baseball, or bowling); vertical jolting (while riding a horse); or stretching your legs strenuously (when hiking or in order to balance a sailboat during a race). On the other hand, if your back feels fine, there's no reason not to pursue these activities—in moderation. Just make sure you listen for when your body says, "Enough!"

It's also important to note that exercising to an extreme can have a deleterious effect on your bones and—ultimately—on your back, especially for women. Studies have shown conclusively that women who exercise intensively and strenuously to the point of not menstruating lose calcium from their bones and thereby heighten their risk for osteoporosis and other spinal problems later in life.

Getting in the Exercise Groove

The most import aspect of exercise is to do it! This is not so easy for some of us. If you're a dedicated exerciser, skip this paragraph. But for the rest of us, here are some tips that have helped me and my patients to get—and stay—in the exercise groove.

- Pick activities you enjoy.
- Commit to a regular schedule.

- Make sure your exercise equipment is accessible, with equipment permanently set up at home or through membership at a gym close to work or home. (Confession: I belong to two gyms, one near my office and another in a YMCA near where I live. And I have an exercise bike in the basement of my house. An indulgence? For sure, but one that I value because I have exercise options close by on weekdays, weekends, and holidays, and at all times of day.)
- Enlist the support and help of your family; for example, spouses can alternate taking care of small children so the other can go to the gym.
- Recruit family members or friends to exercise and have fun with you on bike rides, walks, or outings to the pool.

Join a Gym or Go It Alone?

You don't need to join a gym to maintain a healthy back; you can do all the exercises and activities just fine on your own. Plus at home, you needn't worry about how you look to others or whether you'll have time to make it to the gym. And most people will agree that money saved by not paying for a gym can be put to good use elsewhere, whether that means monthly bills or a new exercise bike.

But there's another side to the gym story. While gym memberships can be costly, a well-run facility offers certain advantages. The cost alone can be an incentive to exercise regularly. Classes offer companionship and a safe way to learn technique, provided the classes are geared toward your back's needs and your ability level. Some people find companionship helps motivate them. Often, personal trainers are available to make sure you're using the equipment appropriately and to suggest ways to make your exercise program more interesting. And some gyms offer a post-workout sauna, steam room, or whirlpool that can serve as a relaxing reward.

Don't Let Cost Be a Barrier

If the cost of gym membership deters you from exercising, YMCA/YWCA branches, community centers, and even local boys and girls clubs often offer adult memberships at reasonable prices. Your health insurance plan or employer might provide a discount for a health club membership. Working out during off-peak hours can cut costs. Some facilities also let you choose to forgo certain amenities, such as the whirlpool and sauna, shower room, or certain classes. Seniors can often find low-cost or free exercise classes through their local council on aging or senior center.

Watch Your Weight

Although carrying too much weight per se has not been proven to be a primary cause of back disorders, extra pounds increase the risk your back pain will return. The heavier you are, the greater the load your spine must carry. To make matters worse, if the bulk of your weight comes in the form of abdominal fat, rather than muscle, your center of gravity can shift forward—a condition that puts added pressure on your back. By maintaining a healthy weight, you can ease the burden on your spine.

To determine a healthy target weight for you, see Table 10.1. To use this table, find your height in the first column. Move across to your weight. The number at the intersection of your height and weight is your body mass index (BMI). The BMI takes both your height and weight into consideration. Not only will you help your

Table 10.1
Body Mass Index

Height	Weight															
	100	110	120	130	140	150	160	170	180	190	200	210	220	230	240	250
5'0"	20	21	23	25	27	29	31	33	35	37	39	41	43	45	47	49
5'1"	19	21	23	25	26	28	30	32	34	36	38	40	42	43	45	47
5'2"	18	20	22	24	26	27	29	31	33	35	37	38	40	42	44	46
5'3"	18	19	21	23	25	27	28	30	32	34	35	37	39	41	43	44
5'4"	17	19	21	22	24	26	27	29	31	33	34	36	38	39	41	43
5'5"	17	18	20	22	23	25	27	28	30	32	33	35	37	38	40	42
5'6"	16	18	19	21	23	24	26	27	29	31	32	34	36	37	39	40
5'7"	16	17	19	20	22	23	25	27	28	30	31	33	34	36	38	39
5'8"	15	17	18	20	21	23	24	26	27	29	30	32	33	35	36	38
5'9"	15	16	18	19	21	22	24	25	27	28	30	31	32	34	35	37
5'10"	14	16	17	19	20	22	23	24	26	27	29	30	32	33	34	36
5'11"	14	15	17	18	20	21	22	24	25	26	27	28	30	32	33	35
6'0"	14	15	16	18	19	20	22	23	24	26	27	28	30	31	33	34
6'1"	13	15	16	17	18	20	21	22	24	25	26	28	29	30	32	33
6'2"	13	14	15	17	18	19	21	22	23	24	26	27	28	30	31	32
6'3"	12	14	15	16	17	19	20	21	22	24	25	26	27	29	30	31
6'4"	12	13	15	16	17	18	19	21	22	23	24	26	27	28	29	30

BMI Interpretation

Under 19	Underweight
19–25	Normal
26–29	Overweight
30 and above	Obese

back if you maintain a normal BMI (in the range of 19–25), but you'll also lower your risk for many diseases, including heart attack, stroke, diabetes, and high blood pressure.

Kick the Smoking Habit

Smoking harms your health. I know you've heard this message before, but smoking not only increases your risk for lung cancer, heart disease, hypertension, and a plethora of other health problems, it also jeopardizes your back. Smokers have more frequent episodes of back pain and the number of episodes increases the more people smoke.

Scientists believe that the nicotine in cigarettes contributes to low-back pain in two ways. First, nicotine hampers the flow of blood to the vertebrae and intervertebral disks. This impairs their function and may trigger a bout of back pain. Second, smokers tend to lose bone faster than nonsmokers, putting them at greater risk for osteoporosis.

While smoking certainly plays a role in low-back pain, it's not known whether it's a primary cause or a contributing factor. But in any event, one thing is clear: smoking is bad news for backs.

The Everyday Business of Moving and Sitting

Everyday activities, from vacuuming your house to sitting in front of the computer for hours, can take a toll on your back, particularly if you aren't schooled in proper body mechanics. Without knowing it, you may be encouraging a return of neck and back pain by the way you perform everyday activities. Look at how you do the basic tasks of life and consider making some changes to safeguard your back.

Back-Smart Lifting

Whenever you need to lift even a moderately heavy object:

- Face the object and position yourself close to it.
- Bend at your knees, not your waist, and squat down as far as you comfortably can.
- Tighten your stomach and keep your buttocks tucked in.
- Lift with your legs, not your back muscles.
- Don't try to lift the object too high. Don't raise a heavy load any higher than your waist; keep a light load below shoulder level.
- Keep the object close to you as you lift it.
- If you need to turn to set something down, don't twist your upper body. Instead, turn your entire body, moving your shoulders, hips, and feet at the same time.
- Ask for help with lifting anything that's too heavy.

Backpacks: Lighten Your Load

Like the itinerant snail, many of us carry much of our homes on our backs in weighty backpacks as we go about our day. But an overstuffed backpack can put you at risk for low-back, upper-back, and shoulder pain. We see this more and more in children and students. Hauling an overloaded backpack can cause muscle fatigue and strain and encourage the wearer to bend forward unnaturally.

If you use a backpack, take the following steps to protect yourself:

- Use both the pack's straps instead of slinging one strap over a shoulder.
- Carry only the essentials, and lighten your load whenever possible.
- Select backpacks that have different-sized compartments to help distribute weight more evenly, and look for wide, padded straps, a hip strap, and a padded back.
- When carrying a heavy load, put the heaviest items as close as possible to the center of the back, and use the hip strap for support. For very heavy loads use a backpack with wheels.
- Remember to bend from your knees when picking up your pack.

Sitting Correctly at Your Computer

When working at the computer or even just working at a desk, your goal should be to keep your head balanced directly over your spine as much as possible and your lower back supported. That means setting a chair height so that both feet can rest on the ground and sitting with your buttocks far back in your chair, using a small pillow to support your lower back if needed. (For more tips, see Figure 10.1.) Your arms should hang freely at your side so that you don't need to use your shoulder and upper back muscles to support them. Your forearms and thighs should both be parallel to the floor. You can see from Figure 10.1 that proper positioning means having the monitor placed at the level of your eyes and the keyboard at the level of your belly button. Getting the monitor at the right height is usually easy. Put an old telephone directory underneath it if it's too low. The keyboard height is trickier and usually requires a keyboard tray. You can also see that properly adjusting the keyboard and monitor positions will be impossible with a laptop computer. Laptop users should buy a separate, full-size keyboard to help achieve better positioning.

Never hold the telephone between your head and shoulder. Use your hands, a headset model, or a speakerphone.

Keep your upper back and neck straight and your head positioned directly over your neck.

Use armrests to support your forearms.

Slide your buttocks far back in your chair.

Set your chair height so you can keep both feet flat on the ground.

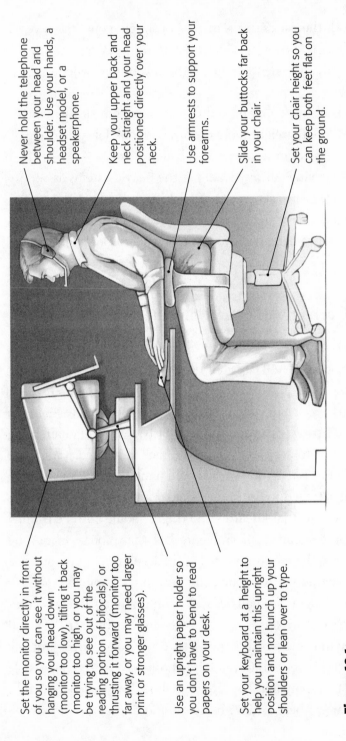

Set the monitor directly in front of you so you can see it without hanging your head down (monitor too low), tilting it back (monitor too high, or you may be trying to see out of the reading portion of bifocals), or thrusting it forward (monitor too far away, or you may need larger print or stronger glasses).

Use an upright paper holder so you don't have to bend to read papers on your desk.

Set your keyboard at a height to help you maintain this upright position and not hunch up your shoulders or lean over to type.

Figure 10.1

Desk Posture

Set up your chair, desk, and computer in ways that are healthy for your neck and back.

No matter how perfect your office-chair posture, it's important to get up, stretch, and move around *every half hour*. The same is true if you have to stand in the same position for a long period. Stretch, shift your position, or take a short walk when you can.

Setting Up Your Work Space. Choose an office chair that offers good back support, preferably with an adjustable backrest, lumbar support, armrests, and wheels. (Some people find armrests uncomfortable.) And set up your work space so you don't have to do a lot of twisting. Experiment before you make your choice. Use an upright paper holder so you don't have to bend to read something sitting flat on your desk. For noncomputer desk work, adjust the chair and desk (blocks may help) so you needn't bend over to write. Paper can also be held on a slant board that raises it slightly off the desk and keeps it at a comfortable angle.

Talking on the Telephone. If you spend a lot of time on the phone, check your neck position. A headset or a speakerphone is a good option for hands-free talking. Also, keep the phone nearby, not at the outer edge of the desk, so you don't have to do contortions to reach the phone.

Reading Comfortably. Sit up straight and position your book so you don't need to bend over. Armrests, a desk document holder, or a pillow on your lap may help. If you must read in bed, sit up straight or use a specially designed wedge pillow.

Driving Tips

While driving, sit back in your seat, and if your seat doesn't provide sufficient support, place a blanket or some towels behind your lower back. Try to shift your weight occasionally. If you have a cruise control feature, use it when you can. Also consider using a foam seat cushion to absorb some of the vibration. Make frequent stops when driving long distances.

Your posture is also a factor in whether a crash will cause whiplash. To work properly, your headrest should be high enough and close enough to catch your head in a rear-end collision. Position

Back Belts: Not a Panacea

Back belts have gained in popularity among workers who must often lift goods—from grocery store clerks to nurses' aides to airline baggage handlers. With back problems accounting for nearly 20 percent of all workplace injuries in the United States and costing anywhere from $20–$50 billion a year (costs are high in other countries, too), it's no surprise that some companies require their workers to use these belts.

But most studies cast doubt on whether back belts can protect workers' backs or reduce sick time and workers' compensation claims. And although a few studies have found them to be protective, the consensus is that back belts do not reduce back injuries. The U.S. National Institute of Occupational Safety and Health (NIOSH) has expressed concern that these belts may even do harm by giving workers a false sense of security. According to NIOSH, there is evidence that workers think they can lift heavier items when wearing the belts. NIOSH also points out that there is no scientific evidence to back up claims that these belts decrease the force exerted on the spine, that they remind wearers to lift properly, or that they reduce workplace injuries. As a result, the agency doesn't recommend that employers insist that their workers use back belts to prevent back injuries.

the seat so you can sit up straight with your head no more than two to four inches in front of the headrest. Adjust the headrest so its upper edge is level with the top of your head: the back curve of your skull should meet the cushion of the headrest.

House and Garden Tips

While standing to perform ordinary household tasks like ironing or folding laundry, keep one foot on a small step stool. If sitting is more comfortable, keep your knees a bit higher than your hips and bend them at a 90-degree angle. Sit with your feet comfortably on the floor. If your feet don't reach the floor, put a book or a small stool under them. Because vacuuming can take a toll on your back, tackle rooms in chunks, vacuuming for no more than five to ten minutes at a time.

If you're an avid gardener, use tools that allow you to stand upright; squat and kneel instead of bending from the waist; and weed and dig when the ground is moist and soft. If bending over is very uncomfortable, consider having raised beds installed in your garden area. They'll allow you to garden standing up. I don't recommend back belts for leisure or work activities.

Although there's no absolute guarantee you won't have a repeat episode of back pain, the activities I've outlined in this chapter will go a long way to nipping a resurgent problem in the bud. There are, however, a few people for whom back pain is something they live with every day. But even for these unfortunate people, there are ways of coping with persistent back pain and living productive and fulfilling lives. We'll address how in Chapter 11.

Chapter 11

When Pain Persists

Chances are you're reading this chapter because you're one of the unfortunate few whose back pain has persisted for months—possibly years; or maybe you're worried because your back pain hasn't cleared up as quickly as you'd hoped it would.

Most back pain attributable to sprain-and-strain and disk syndromes is self-limiting; it will go away on its own over time. But for a small number of people, the pain persists and severely affects the quality of their lives.

Pain That Takes on a Life of Its Own

The reasons why acute back pain, which comes on suddenly, evolves into chronic pain (lasting more than six months) are complex. The phenomenon relates to the perception of pain in the brain I described in Chapter 6. In *acute pain*, the peripheral nervous system sends messages from where you hurt (such as a herniated disk at L4–5) to the central nervous system (spinal cord and brain), where the information is processed and perceived as pain. In *chronic pain*, the role of the peripheral nervous system is much less important and the central nervous system becomes much more important. Put simply, in chronic pain, neurophysiologic changes occur in the brain, which in essence alter pain perception. If we think back to the backyard sensor light analogy I used in Chapter 6, the pain sensor switch is now stuck in the "on" position with no way to turn it off. Pain has taken on a life of its own that is no longer anatomically faithful to the original injury. Indeed, for some patients, where and how they feel pain no longer makes anatomical sense. Is the patient imagining his or her pain? No. The pain these patients feel is only too real. The challenge becomes how to help them lead active and meaningful lives, while not necessarily becoming pain free because that may not be possible.

What Is Debilitating Chronic Pain?

Earlier in the book I defined chronic pain as pain lasting six months or more. But duration isn't the only aspect of debilitating persistent pain. It also involves physical, affective (mood), and social features that accumulate as a result of the pain. The multiple dimensions of chronic pain make this a very difficult syndrome to treat. Patients stop doing activities and become deconditioned. They can become depressed, hostile, angry, and anxious because the pain they feel wears down their patience and interferes with the roles they play in the home, at work, and in society. Unable to work, they may wander around the house irritable, not able to do much, spending more time with spouses and children. This may sound cozy but is typically a formula for disaster. As one of my patients said of her recently retired husband: "I said for better and I said for worse, but I never said for lunch!"

Back-related unemployment puts economic strain on the household budget and makes patients feel valueless because they aren't providing for their families. Patients may also be in the very difficult position of fighting for disability benefits, which involves proving they're not fit to work, at the very time they're trying to get well. Some patients find this dynamic difficult to manage. When all these features are tallied—diminished physical capability, reduced standing in the family and society, reduced income, and increased financial stress—it's a lot to handle.

Who's at Risk?

The overall number of back patients who develop chronic back pain is low. Only about 1 percent of patients with acute sprain-and-strain and about 1 percent of those with sciatica go on to develop the syndrome. Spinal stenosis patients tend not to develop the psychological and social features of the chronic pain syndrome, perhaps because the problem occurs at a later time in their lives when fewer people depend on them. Thus spinal stenosis patients experience less loss of social role.

Although the overall numbers are low, the cost to individuals, their families, employers, and society is very high. The major reason for such a high cost is that chronic back-pain sufferers tend to be people who are currently in the workforce or who are of working age. When looked at from this perspective, the numbers are startling. Up to 10 percent of workers' compensation claimants with acute low-back pain develop chronic low-back pain. And this 10 percent of claimants accounts for a whopping 90 percent of the national medical and productivity costs of chronic low-back pain.

Interestingly, this pattern is the same in the United States, the United Kingdom, and Canada.

If we know that a relatively small number of working-age adults in their middle years (forties and fifties) are more likely than others to develop debilitating chronic back pain, can we predict who might be at risk and help them sooner? Several physical, biological, psychological, social, and economic risk factors for chronic low-back pain have been identified. They are:

- **Physical.** People who have jobs that require bending and lifting.

- **Biological.** People who have congenital or degenerative back disease, failed back surgery (10 percent of all disk surgeries are unsuccessful), or had repeat surgery; who have widespread pain; who have other chronic pain diseases; or who have less physical function one month after the onset of acute pain.

- **Psychological.** People with poor coping skills; who cope passively (accept their limitations) rather than actively (find ways around their limitations); who view their pain as a catastrophe; who are depressed, distressed, and anxious; who avoid doing things in case it hurts (fear avoidance); or who believe they are generally in poor health. I should note here that even people who typically have adequate coping skills can lose them as their role in the family and society diminishes owing to incapacitating back pain.

- **Social.** People who don't find their job satisfying; who feel underpaid; who aren't supported by their supervisors and coworkers; or who find their work environment stressful, but lack the education or training to move on.

- **Economic.** People who see a disability benefit as a way out of a stressful work situation and so don't have an incentive to get better. On the other hand, if used creatively, a disability benefit can lead to a better life. I tell my patients to treat their time on disability as a paid sabbatical, an opportunity to retrain for a different (possibly higher paying) career. For example, they could switch from a physical occupation to a computer-related occupation. This is a challenging prescription, especially for patients with limited education or literacy. But with a change of thinking, paid time off represents an opportunity to turn a personal tragedy into an opportunity for patients to follow their dreams.

What Can Be Done for Patients with Chronic Pain?

Despite being a difficult syndrome to treat, much can be done to improve the quality of life of patients with chronic back pain. First, though, patients need to shift their focus away from the notion that once their pain is gone they'll be able to get on with their lives. Their pain may never completely go, but that doesn't mean they can't get on with their lives. The focus now becomes "functional restoration," or how to enable patients to become more limber, stronger, and physically conditioned so they can do the things that matter to them. Most patients can't achieve this on their own and few primary care doctors have the knowledge to guide patients through the process. Functional restoration requires a highly qualified team of professionals from a number of medical specialties working with the patient. Such teams are found in medical centers, and patients need to be referred to them or seek them out for themselves.

How Chronic Pain Teams Work

A team typically consists of a pain-management specialist, a physiotherapist, and a psychologist. The pain-management specialist understands the complex pharmacology of pain relief and will find the medication combination that works for you. This may include using opiates; medications that work on the central nervous system, such as antiseizure medications (gabapentin, trade name Neurontin) and antidepressants (amitriptyline, trade name Elavil and others); analgesics and NSAIDs; and occasionally epidural and trigger point injections. There are also sophisticated systems for delivering medicine such as indwelling pumps. The physiotherapist will immediately get to work conditioning you because by now you're probably very deconditioned and weak. At some point you may simulate the activities you need to return to your work environment, known as "work hardening." The psychologist will help you cope with negative feelings associated with chronic pain.

With an experienced team working with you to restore your ability to function in your usual roles, you're going to feel better because you'll start doing things you thought you could no longer do. And this is how you track your progress: by appreciating what you can do rather than the pain you feel. One is hope; the other is hopeless. It is indeed possible to turn a bad situation around. I see it every day. So let me end this chapter and this book with the real-life, hope-filled stories of two of my patients, Phil and Theresa, whom you met in earlier chapters.

Phil, as you recall, has congenital spinal stenosis. By the time I met him he had undergone three lumbar fusion surgeries. At that time, Phil was in constant pain and finding his life very difficult to manage. Ruling out further surgery, Phil and I embarked on a quest to have Phil living the life he envisioned. Today Phil is on a complex regimen to manage his pain. He takes an opiate, an antiseizure medication, Tylenol, and an NSAID. He exercises regularly; he has acupuncture every couple of weeks; he paces himself. Phil leads a full and active life. He's a happily married, productive professional and is a source of support to many people.

Theresa, whom you met in Chapter 1, struggled with chronic back pain for years. This made it very difficult for her to do the activities she liked. In fact, her fear of hurting herself developed into fear avoidance, meaning she would avoid many physical movements just in case they hurt. Fear avoidance quickly leads to diminished range of motion and muscle weakness, so Theresa found herself getting nowhere fast. Refusing to accept this situation, she worked with a psychologist who helped her recognize her behavior around her pain. Once Theresa saw how she was holding back, she was able to work very hard with a physical therapist and regain some of her range of motion, strength, and flexibility. She now leads a much more active life.

My final point is that both Phil and Theresa deal with some degree of pain every day. They don't, however, permit their pain to imprison them. By actively engaging in their therapy and working in partnership with a team to identify the best combination of exercises, medications, and other therapies, they lead the fulfilling lives they hoped for.

If you are suffering from back pain, be it acute or chronic, my hope is the same for you. Engage in your therapy, stick with it, and give yourself the life that matters to you.

Glossary

ankylosing spondylitis: An inflammatory disease of the spine that often leads to painful alterations of the vertebral articulations as well as to stiffness of the spine.

annulus fibrosus: The tough multilayered, fibrous outer portion of each intervertebral disk.

articular processes: The two superior and two inferior bony processes on the back part of each vertebra that form the facet joints.

atlas: Another name for the C-1 vertebra of the neck, which lies at the base of the skull.

axis: Another name for the C-2 vertebra of the neck, which lies just beneath C-1.

bone scan: A diagnostic procedure in which radioactive material is injected into the patient's bloodstream to produce images of the bony skeleton. Used to evaluate if and where there is rapid bone formation due to, for example, a tumor or an infection.

cauda equina: The bundle of nerve roots that starts where the true spinal cord ends in the upper lumbar spine, traverses down the spinal canal in the lumbar and sacral regions, and terminates in the lower sacrum.

cervical radiculopathy: Compression of the spinal nerve roots in the neck, causing neurological dysfunction such as weakness and reduced sensation, as well as symptoms such as tingling and numbness in the areas served by the nerves.

cervical spine: The top seven vertebrae of the spine.

chemonucleolysis: A treatment for low-back pain that involves injecting the enzyme chymopapain into a herniated disk to dissolve the nucleus pulposus.

coccyx: The final four fused vertebrae of the spine; also called the "tailbone."

compression fracture: The collapse and fracture of a bone, most often a vertebra. Most often seen in people with osteoporosis.

computed tomography (CT): A diagnostic technique in which x-rays are taken in many different directions. A computer synthesizes the x-rays to generate cross-sectional and other images of the body.

degenerative disk disease: A general term for the age-related deterioration (loss of water and increased brittleness) of the cushioning disks between the vertebrae.

degenerative joint disease: A joint disease common with aging that is characterized by progressive deterioration of the cartilage lining the joints; also called "osteoarthritis."

disk: See *intervertebral disk.*

diskectomy: The surgical removal of all or part of an intervertebral disk.

diskitis: Inflammation of an intervertebral disk.

electromyography (EMG): A series of diagnostic procedures in which electrical activity in muscles is measured to help diagnose neuromuscular disorders.

facet joint: The paired joints located on the back side of each vertebra, connecting its posterior elements to those of the vertebrae above and below. Facet joints can be a source of back pain.

fibromyalgia syndrome: Collection of symptoms including painful tender points, especially in the muscles of the upper neck, shoulders, hips, and lower back.

free fragment: A displaced portion of an intervertebral disk that has become detached from the central portion of the disk.

herniated disk: Displacement of some portion of the disk out of its normal location; sometimes indicates a ruptured or slipped disk.

iliopsoas muscles: Two muscles, each of which is located on and attached to each side of the lumbar vertebrae as well as being attached to the inside of the pelvis and to the thighbone.

intervertebral disk: One of the small, energy-absorbing cushions located between the vertebrae of the spine.

intervertebral foramen: The opening between vertebrae through which a spinal nerve (nerve root) exits the spinal column (plural: foramina).

intradiscal electrothermal annuloplasty (IDET): A procedure to relieve the pain of certain disk problems, in which a heated catheter—inserted via a needle placed in the affected disk—sears or cauterizes the nerve fibers along the disk wall.

kyphoplasty: A minimally invasive procedure to alleviate pain from spinal compression fractures. An orthopedic balloon is placed in the affected vertebra and inflated; the resulting cavity is filled with bone cement to stabilize the vertebral fracture.

kyphosis: An abnormal curvature of the mid-to-upper spine that can result from compression fractures of vertebrae. Commonly called "dowager's hump."

lamina: One of the two thin, platelike parts of each vertebra that join in the midline and form the base of the spinous process of that vertebra (plural: laminae).

laminectomy: An operation in which all or part of one or both laminae is removed to gain access to the spinal canal or to decompress the spinal cord and nerve roots.

ligament: Fibrous tissue that stabilizes and connects bones.

lumbar spinal stenosis: A reduction in the size of the spinal canal, which may result in compression of nerve roots in the lumbar area.

lumbar spine: The five lowest mobile vertebrae of the spine.

magnetic resonance imaging (MRI): A diagnostic technique in which radio waves generated in a strong magnetic field are used to provide information about the hydrogen atoms in different tissues within the body; a computer uses this information to pro-duce images of the tissues in many different planes.

microdiskectomy: Similar to standard diskectomy but involving a smaller incision.

myelography: A diagnostic technique in which x-rays are taken of the spine after a contrast medium has been injected into the space within the sheath that surrounds the spinal cord and the cauda equina. This test enables a radiologist to see distortions in the shape of the space (produced by problems such as a herniated disk, tumor, fracture, or spinal stenosis).

myelopathy: Compression of the spinal cord.

myofascial pain syndrome: Painful trigger points where muscle and fascia (connective tissue) meet.

nucleus pulposus: The gel-like central portion of each intervertebral disk.

osteoarthritis: A joint disease common with aging that is characterized by progressive deterioration of the cartilage lining the joints; also called "degenerative joint disease."

osteophyte: An outgrowth of bone on the margins of a joint or intervertebral disk, commonly called a "bone spur," generally a result of osteoarthritis.

osteoporosis: A degenerative disease that decreases the density of bone, leaving it vulnerable to compression fractures.

percutaneous diskectomy: A less invasive technique than standard diskectomy that removes part of an intervertebral disk by means of a narrow probe inserted through the skin and muscle of the back.

ruptured disk: See *herniated disk*.

sacrum: The five fused vertebrae between the lumbar spine and coccyx. The number of vertebrae can vary.

sciatica: Pain along the course of the sciatic nerve (from the buttock, down the back and side of the leg, and into the foot and toes), often due to a herniated disk.

slipped disk: See *herniated disk*.

spinal fusion: Joining two or more vertebrae with a bone graft or other technique in order to eliminate motion and relieve pain.

spinous process: The handle-like backward bony projection from each vertebra, to which muscles and ligaments are attached (plural: processes).

spondylolisthesis: Forward displacement (slippage) of one vertebra over the vertebra immediately below.

spondylosis: A general term for degeneration of the spine that causes narrowing of the spinal canal and the intervertebral foramina through which spinal nerves exit the canal.

sprain: Injury to a ligament that may involve overstretching and the development of small tears.

standard diskectomy: The surgical removal of all or part of an intervertebral disk through an incision, which allows the surgeon to see the extent of the problem; also called "open back surgery."

strain: Injury to a muscle caused by misuse or overuse.

tendon: Fibrous tissue connecting muscle and bone.

thoracic spine: The twelve vertebrae between the cervical and lumbar spine.

transcutaneous electrical nerve stimulation (TENS): Use of low-voltage electrical current to provide pain-suppressing stimulation.

transverse processes: The ringlike projection on each side of a vertebra to which muscles and ligaments are attached and, in the chest area, to which the ribs are connected.

trapezius muscle: Large posterior neck muscle; one of the most common sites of neck pain.

trigger point: A painful area that when stimulated also elicits pain elsewhere in the body—such as the arm, shoulder, hip, leg, or another area of the back.

vertebra: One of the cylindrical bones that form the spine (plural: vertebrae).

vertebroplasty: A minimally invasive procedure to stabilize compressed vertebrae and alleviate pain. A needle is inserted into the compressed portion of a vertebra and surgical cement is injected into it.

whiplash: The popular term for muscle and ligament damage resulting from rapid and extreme extension and flexion of the neck. The term is also used for the accident causing the injury—most often a rear-end motor vehicle accident.

Additional Resources

Organizations

American Academy of Orthopaedic Surgeons
6300 N. River Road
Rosemont, IL 60018
847-823-7186
aaos.org

This professional organization for orthopedic surgeons provides patient education information on neck and back problems. The website includes a physician locator.

American Academy of Physical Medicine and Rehabilitation
330 N. Wabash Avenue, Suite 2500
Chicago, IL 60611
312-464-9700
aapmr.org

This professional organization for physiatrists, doctors who specialize in physical medicine and rehabilitation for musculoskeletal and neurological problems, provides information on a variety of conditions such as low-back and neck pain, spinal cord and brain injuries, osteoporosis, and arthritis. The website includes a physician locator.

American College of Rheumatology
1800 Century Place, Suite 250
Atlanta, GA 30345
404-633-3777
rheumatology.org

This professional organization for specialists in arthritis and related conditions provides patient education on back pain, fibromyalgia, and several types of arthritis. The website includes a physician locator.

American Council on Exercise

4851 Paramount Drive
San Diego, CA 92123
800-825-3636
acefitness.org

This nonprofit organization promotes fitness and a healthy lifestyle. ACE certifies fitness professionals and also offers educational materials and consumer information on locating a health club and a personal trainer.

American Chronic Pain Association

P.O. Box 850
Rocklin, CA 95677
800-533-3231
theacpa.org

This association provides information and support for people with chronic pain. Membership includes a year's subscription to the association's newsletter and 10 percent off all other materials ordered from the association.

American Massage Therapy Association

500 Davis Street, Suite 900
Evanston, IL 60201
877-905-2700
amtamassage.org

This professional association for massage therapists offers a therapist locator service on its website.

American Pain Foundation
201 N. Charles Street, Suite 710
Baltimore, MD 21201
888-615-7246
painfoundation.org

This nonprofit organization serves as an information clearinghouse and resource center for people with pain, including back pain.

American Physical Therapy Association
1111 N. Fairfax St.
Alexandria, VA 22314
800-999-2782 (toll-free)
apta.org

This national professional organization for physical therapists provides links to related sites. The website includes a physical therapist locator.

Arthritis Foundation
P.O. Box 7669
Atlanta, GA 30357
800-283-7800 (toll-free)
arthritis.org

This nonprofit organization provides up-to-date information on many arthritic conditions as well as on exercise, research, and current treatments. The website includes a physician locator.

Biofeedback Certification Institute of America
10200 W. 44th Avenue, Suite 310
Wheat Ridge, CO 80033
303-420-2902
bcia.org

This professional organization certifies practitioners in biofeedback services and offers general information on biofeedback. The website includes a BCIA-certified practitioner locator.

National Center for Complementary and Alternative Medicine

National Institutes of Health
9000 Rockville Pike
Bethesda, MD 20892
888-644-6226 (toll-free)
TTY: 866-464-3615 (toll-free)
nccam.nih.gov

This government agency provides science-based information on the safety and efficacy of complementary and alternative medicine. Does not provide medical advice for individuals or referrals to practitioners.

National Certification Commission for Acupuncture and Oriental Medicine

11 Canal Center Plaza, Suite 300
Alexandria, VA 22314
703-548-9004
nccaom.org

This nonprofit organization seeks to promote nationally recognized standards of competency and safety in acupuncture, Chinese herbology, and Oriental bodywork therapy. The website includes a certified practitioner locator.

National Osteoporosis Foundation

1232 22nd Street, NW
Washington, DC 20037
202-223-2226
nof.org

This nonprofit organization supports research on osteoporosis and provides educational materials. The website includes a member practitioner locator.

Osteoporosis and Related Bone Diseases–
National Resource Center
National Institutes of Health
2 AMS Circle
Bethesda, MD 20892
800-624-2663
TTY: 202-466-4315
osteo.org

This government organization is dedicated to increasing awareness of osteoporosis, Paget's disease, osteogenesis imperfecta, and hyperparathyroidism. The center provides health professionals and the general public with information about these conditions and their treatment, as well as links to other resources.

Spine-health.com
123 West Madison Street, Suite 1450
Chicago, IL 60602
spine-health.com

This commercial website provides in-depth information on back pain, including common causes, diagnostic measures, treatments, and surgery. The site also features information on recent advances. Medical professionals review all content.

The National Foundation for the Treatment of Pain
P.O. Box 70045
Houston, TX 77270
916-725-5669
paincare.org

This organization supports individuals who have intractable pain and medical and legal professionals who work with people who have legitimate medical pain.

DVDs

Yoga for the Rest of Us
Peggy Cappy

A step-by-step gentle yoga program for people of all ages and abilities. Includes stretches, breathing, and poses that can be done with or without the support of a chair, and relaxation. DVD includes closed captions.

More Yoga for the Rest of Us
Peggy Cappy

A step-by-step gentle yoga program for people of all ages and abilities. Includes stretches, breathing, and another series of poses that can be done with or without the support of a chair, and relaxation. DVD includes closed captions.

Index

Abdominal muscles, 48, 49
Acetaminophen (Tylenol)
  brand names containing, 122
  defined, 117, 118–19
  liver damage and, 120
  opioids with, 123, 127
Acupuncture, 143, 152–54
Acute back pain
  bed rest and, 180–81
  chronic versus, 14, 106, 239–40
  cold and heat for, 178–80
  defined, 106
  low-impact aerobic exercises for, 201–2,
    226
  resting your lower back and, 182
  resting your neck and, 181
  waiting out, 177–78
Aerobic exercises, low-impact
  acute back pain and, 201–2
  for prevention of back problems, 226
Age, as risk factor, 18–19
Aleve (naproxen sodium), 117, 118–19, 122
Alexander technique, 165–66
Alternative medicine, defined, 144
Amitriptyline (Elavil, Endep), 128, 244
Anatomy
  five spinal regions, 37, 38
  letters and numbers system of vertebrae,
    39
  lower-back, 45–49
  neck, 39–44
  sacrum and coccyx, 38, 50
  thoracic spine, 38, 50
Anatomy, lower-back
  cauda equina, 45, 46, 47, 48
  cross-sectional view, 46
  lumbar spine, defined, 38, 45
  muscles, 48, 49
  sagittal view, 46
Anatomy, neck
  definition of cervical spine, 37, 38,
    39–40
  facet joints, 41, 42
  intervertebral disks, 42

  muscles, 42–43, 44
  tendons and ligaments, 43–44
  vertebrae, 40–42
Ankylosing spondylitis
  defined, 75
  fibromyalgia and, 61
  frequency and risk of, 56–57
  gender and, 20
  genes and, 21
  symptoms of, 75
Annulus fibrosus, 46
Anticonvulsants, 128–29
Antidepressants, 112, 126, 128, 244
Arthritis of the spine, 75. See also
  Osteoarthritis
Artificial disks, 219–20
Aspirin
  brand names for, 122
  defined, 117, 118–19
  stomach upset and, 120
  willow bark and, 170, 171
Atlas, 40, 41
Axis, 40, 41
Axon, 109

Back belts, 236
Back pain. See also Acute back pain;
  Chronic back pain
  acute versus chronic, 14, 106, 239–40
  as bewildering condition, 4–8
  describing your, 113–14
  factors affecting who gets, 17–25
  factors associated with, 15–16
  location of, 11
  natural history of, 14, 178–79
  patient-centered management of, 10–11
  pervasiveness of , 8–9, 17, 18
  research on, 6–7, 15
  type of, 11–14
  as umbrella term, 10
Back-pain descriptions. See also Causes of
  back pain
  acute, 106
  bone pain, 116

261

chronic, 106
facet joint pain, 115
headache, 115
muscle pain, 114
muscle spasms, 114–15
nerve pain, 115
referred pain, 77, 115–16
subacute, 106
tender points, 114
three types of, 106
trigger points, 114
Back-pain medications
delivery methods for, 129–36
over-the-counter (OTC), 116–21
prescription pain relievers, 121, 123–29
Back surgery
compression (osteoporotic) fractures
and, 214–17
criteria for, 206
disk disease and, 208–14
dislocations and vertebral fractures and,
222
elective, 203–4
infections and, 220–21
laminectomy, 205, 209
lumbar spinal stenosis and, 217–18
readiness for, 222–23
risks and benefits of, 206–8
spinal fusion, 218–20
tumors and, 221
usefulness of, 204
Backpacks, 232–33
Bacterial infections of the spine
description of, 75–76
frequency and risk of, 56–57
surgery for, 220–21
Bed rest, 180–81
Beds, 182, 183
Benson, Dr. Herbert, 155
Biking, 201, 202, 226
Biofeedback, 162–64
Bionic backs, 219–20
Blood tests, 97
Body mass index (BMI), 229–31
Bone pain, 116
Bone scans, 95–96
BOTOX (botulinum toxin), 136
Breath of life, 155–57
Bridge exercise, 200

Capsaicin, 130
Carotid artery dissection, 148
Carrage, Eugene J., 7
Cat stretch, 199

Cauda equina, defined, 45–48, 65
Cauda equina syndrome
description of, 13, 65–66
frequency and risk of, 54–55
as red flag condition, 13, 71, 72
symptoms of, 55, 66
Causes of back pain
degenerative disk conditions, 63–70
degenerative spinal disease, 54–55,
70–71
fibromyalgia syndrome, 56–57, 61–62
fractures, 56–57
infection, 56–57
inflammation, 56–57
myofascial pain syndrome, 56–57, 62
osteoporosis, 73–74
pinched nerve syndromes, 54–55, 63
red flag conditions, 13, 71–72
referred pain and, 77, 115–16
scoliosis, 56–57, 72–73
sprain-and-strain syndromes, 54–55,
58–61
trauma, 56–57, 76
tumors, 56–57, 76
unknown, 56–57
Celebrex (celecoxib), 120, 121
Cervical myelopathy (spinal cord
compression), 54–55, 69
Cervical pain
location of, 11
number of Americans with, 9
pervasiveness of, 8, 9
Cervical radiculopathy (nerve root
compression), 54–55, 68
Cervical spine anatomy
definition of cervical spine, 37, 38,
39–40
facet joints, 41, 42
intervertebral disks, 42
muscles, 42–43, 44
tendons and ligaments, 43–44
vertebrae, 40–42
Cervicogenic headache, 115
Chemonucleolysis, 211, 213–14
Chin retraction (neck muscles), 195
Chiropractic manipulation, 147–48
Chondroitin and glucosamine, 168–69
Chronic back pain
acute versus, 14, 106, 239–40
defined, 106
functional restoration and, 243
multiple dimensions of, 240–41
risk factors for, 241–43
treatment for, 243–45

Chronic pain teams, 243, 244–45
Chymopapain, 211, 213
Clonazepam (Klonopin), 128
Coccyx, 37, 38, 49, 50
Codeine, 123, 125
Cold and heat, 178–80
Complementary exercise programs
    Alexander technique, 165–66
    effectiveness of, 164–65
    Pilates, 166
Complementary/integrative medicine
    (CIM), defined, 145
Complementary medicine, defined,
    144–45
Complementary therapies
    acupuncture, 143, 152–54
    magnets, 167
    massage, 143, 149–51
    mind-body therapies, 154–64
    music and laughter, 167–68
    spinal manipulation, 143, 146–49
Complementary therapist, 145–46
Complete blood count (CBC), 97
Computed tomography (CT) scans, 87, 88,
    91–92
Congenital back diseases, 13
Conventional medicine, defined, 144
COX-2 inhibitors, 119–21
C-reactive protein (CRP) test, 97
Curl up, 197
Cyclooxygenase (COX), 117, 119

Darvocet (propoxyphene and
    acetaminophen), 127
Darvon (propoxyphene), 127
Degenerative disk conditions
    cauda equina syndrome, 13, 54–55,
        65–66, 71, 72
    defined, 63
    frequency and risk of, 54–55
    herniated disk, 54–55, 64, 178–79
    sciatica, 64–65
    spinal stenosis, 54–55, 66–67, 178–79,
        217–18
    spondylolisthesis, 54–55, 67–69, 218
    spondylolysis, 70
    surgery for, 208–14
Degenerative spinal disease
    defined, 70–71
    frequency and risk of, 54–55
Demerol (meperidine), 126
Depression, 23, 128
Desk posture, 22, 233–35
Devil's claw, 170–71

Deyo, Richard A., 7, 176
Diagnosis
    blood tests, 97
    bone scans, 95–96
    computed tomography (CT) scans, 87,
        88, 91–92
    doctors, 81, 82–83, 207
    electromyography (EMG) and nerve
        conduction testing, 96–97
    first step in, 80–81
    imaging tests, 86–95
    magnetic resonance imaging (MRI), 87,
        88, 92–94
    medical history, 83–85
    myelography, 94–95
    physical examination, 85–86
    as process of elimination, 80
    x-rays, 87, 89–90
Diazepam (Valium), 128
Dilaudid (hydromorphone), 125
Disability, 241, 243
Disk bulge, 64
Disk herniation
    description of, 64–65
    frequency and risk of, 54–55
    natural history of, 178–79
Disk protrusion, 64
Diskectomy
    defined, 208
    percutaneous, 210–12
    standard, 209–10
Diskitis
    description of, 75–76
    frequency and risk of, 56–57
    surgery for, 220–21
Doctors
    primary care physicians, 82–83
    surgeons, 207
    when to call, 81
Dolophine (methadone), 126
Dorsal horn, 109
Double hip rotation, 200
Dowager's hump, 73, 74
Driving, 21, 235–37
Drugs for pain relief
    delivery methods, 129–36
    over-the-counter (OTC),
        116–21
    prescription, 121, 123–29

Education, level of, 24
Elavil (amitriptyline), 128, 244
Elbow prop, 198
Elective surgery, 203–4

Electrical stimulation therapies
  percutaneous electrical nerve
    stimulation (PENS), 138
  spinal cord stimulation, 138–39
  transcutaneous electrical nerve
    stimulation (TENS), 112, 113,
    136–38
Electromyography (EMG) and nerve
  conduction testing, 96–97
Endorphins
  defined, 111–12
  laughter and, 168
  low-impact aerobics and, 186, 226
Enkephalin, 111
Epidural steroid injections, 132–33, 134,
    244
Erector spinae, 48, 49
Erythrocyte sedimentation rate, 97
Everyday activities
  back problems and, 231–32
  driving, 21, 235–37
  gardening and housework, 237
  hauling backpacks, 232–33
  lifting heavy objects, 232
  sitting at computer, 22, 233–35
Exercise. See also Mind-body therapies
  aerobic, 201–2, 226
  benefits of, 184
  getting going again, 182–84
  guidelines, 188–90
  prevention of back problems and,
    225–29
  principles of rehabilitative, 186–90
  professional guidance for, 184–85
Exercise programs, complementary
  Alexander technique, 165–66
  effectiveness of, 164–65
  Pilates, 165, 166
Exercises for lower back
  bridge, 200
  cat stretch, 199
  curl up, 197
  double hip rotation, 200
  elbow prop, 198
  lower-back stetch and hip stretch,
    199
  posterior pelvic tilt, 197
  representative selection of, 196
  trunk extension, 198
Exercises for neck
  isometric neck strengtheners,
    190–92
  isotonic neck strengtheners, 192–93
  neck stretches, 193–96

Exercises for shoulder
  shoulder rolls, 196
  shoulder shrug, 196

Facet joint injections, 134, 135
Facet joint pain, 115
Fear avoidance, 23
Fentanyl, 125, 130
Feverfew, 170–71
Fibro fog, 62
Fibromyalgia syndrome
  description of, 61–62
  frequency and risk of, 56–57
  symptoms of, 57, 62
Flexibility and range of motion. See
    also Stretching and strengthening
    exercises
  flexion and extension stretches, 188
  moving neck and back, 186–87
  standing lumbar extension, 189
Fluoroscope, 216
Food and Drug Administration (FDA),
    117
Fractures, osteoporotic
  description of, 73–74
  frequency and risk of, 56–57
  surgery for, 214–17
Free fragment, 209
Functional restoration, 243

Gabapentin (Neurontin), 128–29, 244
Gardening, 237
Gate Control Theory of Pain, 112–13
Gender, as risk factor, 19–20
Genes, 16, 21
Glucocorticoids, 132
Glucosamine and chondroitin, 168–69
Guided imagery, 158, 159
Gym memberships, 228–29

Hamstring stretches, 201
Head rolls, 195–96
Headache, 115
Heat and cold, 178–80
Herbal products, 169–72
Herniated disk (sciatica)
  description of, 64–65
  frequency and risk of, 54–55
  natural history of, 178–79
History, medical, 83–85
Household tasks, 237
Humped back, 73, 74
Hydromorphone (Dilaudid), 125
Hypothalamus, 110

Ibuprofen (Advil, Motrin), 117, 118–19, 122
Ice packs, 179
Iliopsoas muscles, 48, 49
Imagery, guided, 158, 159
Imaging tests
    computed tomography (CT) scans, 87,
        88, 91–92
    cost of, 87, 92
    helpfulness of, 86–89
    magnetic resonance imaging (MRI), 87,
        88, 92–94
    myelography, 94–95
    x-rays, 87, 89–90
Imhotep, 15
Imipramine (Tofranil), 128
Infections of the spine
    description of, 75–76
    frequency and risk of, 56–57
    surgery for, 220–21
Inflammatory spinal arthritis
    description of, 75–76
    frequency and risk of, 56–57
Interventional pain management, 130–31
Intervertebral foramina, 42
Intradiscal electrothermal annuloplasty
    (IDET), 212–13
Isometric neck strengtheners, 190–92

Job dissatisfaction, 15–16, 24, 242
Job-related activities, 21–22, 233–35

Kadian (morphine), 126
Kyphoplasty, 214, 215–16
Kyphosis, 73, 74

Laser diskectomy, 211, 212
Laughter and music, 167–68
Letters and numbers system of vertebrae,
    39
Lidocaine (Lidoderm), 130, 135, 136
Lifestyle factors, 15–16, 21–22
Lifting, back-smart, 232
Liver damage, 120
Location of pain, 11
Low-back pain. *See also* Acute back pain;
    Chronic back pain
    acute versus chronic, 14, 106, 239–40
    as bewildering condition, 4–8
    factors affecting who gets, 17–25
    factors associated with, 15–16
    natural history of, 14, 178–79
    number of Americans with, 8–9, 17, 18
    patient-centered management of, 10–11
    pervasiveness of, 8–9, 17, 18

research on, 6–7, 15
    type of, 11–14
Lower-back anatomy
    cauda equina, 45, 46, 47, 48
    cross-sectional view, 46
    definition of lumbar spine, 38, 45
    muscles, 48, 49
    sagittal view, 46
Lower-back stretching and strengthening
    bridge, 200
    cat stretch, 199
    curl up, 197
    double hip rotation, 200
    elbow prop, 198
    exercise ideas for, 196
    lower-back stretch and hip stretch, 199
    posterior pelvic tilt, 197
    trunk extension, 198
Low-impact aerobic exercise, 201–2, 226
Lumbago, 58
Lumbar pain, 11. *See also* Low-back pain
Lumbar spinal stenosis
    description of, 66–67
    frequency and risk of, 54–55
    natural history of, 178–79
    surgery for, 217–18
Lumbar spine anatomy
    cauda equina, 45, 46, 47, 48
    cross-sectional view, 46
    definition of lumbar spine, 37, 38, 45
    muscles, 48, 49
    sagittal view, 46

Magnetic resonance imaging (MRI), 87,
    88, 92–94
Magnets, 167
Massage, 143, 149–51
Mattresses, 182, 183
Medical history, 83–85
Medical specialists, 82–83
Medications
    delivery methods, 129–36
    over-the-counter (OTC), 116–21
    prescription pain relievers, 121, 123–29
Meditation, 157–58
Meperidine (Demerol), 126
Meridians, 152
Metabolic back disease, 13
Methadone (Dolophine), 126
Microdiskectomy, 210
Mind-body connection, 23–24
Mind-body therapies
    biofeedback, 162–64
    breath of life, 155–57

defined, 154
guided imagery, 158, 159
meditation, 157–58
progressive muscle relaxation, 159–61
relaxation techniques, 154–55
tai chi, 162
yoga, 161–62
Mindfulness meditation, 158
Morphine (MS Contin, Kadian,
      Oramorph), 111, 126
MS Contin (morphine), 126
Muscle pain, 114
Muscle relaxants, 127–28
Muscle spasms, 114–15
Muscle strengthening exercises
isometric neck strengtheners, 190–92
isotonic neck strengtheners, 192–93
lower-back exercises, 196–200
shoulder exercises, 196
Muscles
lumbar spine, 48, 49
neck, 42–43, 44
Music and laughter, 167–68
Myelography, 94–95
Myofascial pain syndrome
description of, 62
frequency and risk of, 56–57
trigger points and, 135

Naproxen sodium (Aleve), 117, 118–19, 122
National Center for Complementary and
      Alternative Medicine (NCCAM),
      146, 167
Natural history of back problem, 14,
      178–79
Neck anatomy
cervical spine, defined, 37, 38, 39–40
facet joints, 41, 42
intervertebral disks, 42
muscles, 42–43, 44
tendons and ligaments, 43–44
vertebrae, 40–42
Neck exercises
isometric neck strengtheners, 190–92
isotonic neck strengtheners, 192–93
neck stretches, 193–96
Neck pain
location of, 11
number of Americans with, 9
pervasiveness of, 8, 9
Nerve blocks, 131–32
Nerve pain, 115
Nerve root compression (cervical
      radiculopathy), 54–55, 68

Nerves and nerve receptors, 108–10
Neurons, 108, 109
Neurontin (gabapentin), 128–29, 244
Neurotransmitters, 23, 108–9, 112, 128
90/90 rest position, 182
Nociceptors, 108
Nonsteroidal anti-inflammatory drugs
      (NSAIDs)
aspirin, 117, 118–19, 120, 122
chronic pain and, 244
COX-2 inhibitors, 119–21
defined, 117–19
herbal products and, 169, 171
Nonsurgical treatments. See also
      Complementary therapies
back's capacity to heal itself, 176–77
bed rest, 180–81
cold and heat, 178–80
low-impact aerobic exercise, 201–2, 226
rehabilitative exercise, 186–90
resting your lower back, 182
resting your neck, 181
sleep, 183
strengthening and stretching muscles,
      190–201
wait-and-watch approach, 175–76
waiting out acute back pain, 177–82
Norepinephrine, 23, 112, 128
Nucleus pulposus, 46

Office work, 21
Office-chair posture, 22, 233–35
Opioids, 123, 125–27
Oramorph (morphine), 126
Osteoarthritis
of facet joints, 54–55, 70–71
glucosamine and chondroitin for,
      168–69
of the spine, 70–71
Osteomyelitis
description of, 75–76
frequency and risk of, 56–57
surgery for, 220–21
Osteopathic medicine, 147
Osteopathy, doctor of, 144
Osteophytes, 63, 66, 67, 70, 71
Osteoporosis
description of, 73–74
frequency and risk of, 56–57
strength training and, 225–26
Osteoporotic fractures
description of, 73–74
frequency and risk of, 56–57
surgery for, 214–17

Over-the-counter (OTC) medications
active ingredients in, 122
labels on, 121
NSAIDs, 117–21
prescription medications versus, 116
Oxycodone (OxyContin), 123, 124, 127
OxyContin, 124, 127

Paget's disease, 66
Pain. *See also* Acute back pain; Chronic
back pain
acute versus chronic, 14, 106, 239–40
defined, 102–3, 105
describing back pain, 113–16
duration of, 106
gate control theory of, 112–13
how pain works, 107–11
perception of, 107
strides in understanding, 103–5
Pain control, golden rule of, 129
Pain descriptions
acute, 106
bone pain, 116
chronic, 106
facet joint pain, 115
headache, 115
muscle pain, 114
muscle spasms, 114–15
nerve pain, 115
referred pain, 77, 115–16
subacute, 106
tender points, 114
three types of, 106
trigger points, 114
Pain medications
delivery methods for, 129–36
over-the-counter (OTC), 116–21
prescription pain relievers, 121,
123–29
Pain relief
body's natural, 111–13
medications, 116–36
three principles of, 110–11
Pain teams, 243, 244–45
Pain treatments, complementary
acupuncture, 143, 152–54
magnets, 167
massage, 143, 149–51
mind-body therapies, 154–64
music and laughter, 167–68
spinal manipulation, 143, 146–49
Pain-management specialists, 244
Patient-centered management, 10–11
Percodan (oxycodone), 123, 127

Percutaneous electrical nerve stimulation
(PENS), 138
Persistent back pain
acute versus, 14, 106, 239–40
defined, 106
functional restoration and, 243
multiple dimensions of, 240–41
risk factors for, 241–43
treatment for, 243–45
Physical examination, 85–86
Physiotherapists, 244
Pilates, 165, 166
Pilates, Joseph, 166
Pinched nerve syndromes
cauda equina syndrome, 13, 54–55,
65–66, 71, 72
cervical myelopathy (spinal cord
compression), 54–55, 69
cervical radiculopathy (nerve root
compression), 54–55, 68
defined, 12
frequency and risk of, 54–55
sciatica (herniated disk), 54–55, 64–65
spinal stenosis, 54–55, 66–67
spondylolisthesis, 20, 21, 54–55
symptoms of, 55
Pituitary gland, 111
Posterior pelvic tilt, 197
Posture, 22, 233–35
Pregnancy, 20–21
Prescription medications
anticonvulsants, 128–29
antidepressants, 126, 128, 244
for chronic or severe pain, 121, 244
muscle relaxants, 127–28
opioids, 123, 125–27
Prevalence of back pain, 8–9
Prevention of back problems
everyday activities and, 231–37
exercising regularly for, 227–29
smoking and, 231
staying fit for, 225–27
watching your weight for, 229–31
Primary care physicians, 82–83
Processes, 33–34
Progressive muscle relaxation, 159–61
Prostaglandins, 117–18
Psychological factors, 23–24
Psychologists, 244, 245

Qi, 152

Radiographs, 87, 89–90
Range of motion, 186–87

Red flag conditions, 13, 71–72
Referred pain, 77, 115–16
Relaxation techniques, 154–55
Research on low-back pain
    first scientific paper, 15
    important reviews of, 6–7
Rest
    bed rest, 180–81
    resting your lower back, 182
    resting your neck, 181
    sleep, 183
Risk factors
    age, 18–19
    education, 24
    gender, 19–20
    genes, 16, 21
    job dissatisfaction, 15–16, 24
    lifestyle factors, 15–16, 21–22
    pregnancy, 20–21
    psychological distress, 23–24
    smoking, 24, 231
Rotational thrust, 148
Ruptured disk, 64. See also Herniated disk
    (sciatica)

Sacrum, 37, 38, 49, 50
Safety guidelines for exercise,
    188–90
Sciatica (herniated disk)
    causes of, 65
    frequency and risk of, 54–55
    natural history of, 178–79
    symptoms of, 64–65
Scoliosis
    description of, 72–73
    frequency and risk of, 56–57
Serotonin, 23, 128, 153
Shoulder stretching and strengthening
    shoulder rolls, 196
    shoulder shrug, 196
Sitting at computer, 22, 233–35
Slipped disk, 64. See also Herniated disk
    (sciatica)
Smoking, 24, 231
Specialists, 82–83
Spinal cord, 45, 47, 48
Spinal cord stimulation, 138–39
Spinal fusion surgery, 218–20
Spinal manipulation, 143, 146–49
Spinal stenosis
    description of, 66–67
    frequency and risk of, 54–55
    natural history of, 178–79
    surgery for, 217–18

Spine
    general description of, 37–38
    letters and numbers system of vertebrae,
        39
    lower-back anatomy, 45–49
    neck anatomy, 39–44
    sacrum and coccyx, 38, 50
    thoracic spine, 38, 50
Spinous processes, 34
Spondylolisthesis
    defined, 67–69
    frequency and risk of, 54–55
    gender and, 20
    genes and, 21
    spinal fusion surgery and, 218
Spondylolysis
    defined, 70
    frequency and risk of, 56–57
    symptoms of, 70
Sprain, defined, 59
Sprain-and-strain syndromes
    defined, 12
    frequency and risk of, 54–55
    natural history of, 178–79
    symptoms of, 55
Standing lumbar extension, 189
Steroid injections, 132
Straight-leg-raising test, 86
Strain, defined, 58–59
Stress, 23–24
Stretching and strengthening exercises
    flexion and extension, 188, 189
    hamstring stretch, 201
    lower-back exercises, 196–200
    neck exercises, 193–96
    shoulder exercises, 196
    standing lumbar extension, 189
Subacute back pain, 106
Surgery
    compression (osteoporotic) fractures
        and, 214–17
    criteria for, 206
    disk disease and, 208–14
    dislocations and vertebral fractures and,
        222
    elective, 203–4
    infections and, 220–21
    laminectomy, 205, 209
    lumbar spinal stenosis and, 217–18
    readiness for, 222–23
    risks and benefits of, 206–8
    spinal fusion, 218–20
    tumors and, 221
    usefulness of, 204

Swimming
 as low-impact exercise, 226
 water therapy, 201, 202
Synapse, 109
Synovial fluid, 34

Tailbone (coccyx), 37, 38, 49, 50
Telephone, talking on, 22, 234, 235
Tender points, 114
Tendons and ligaments
 defined, 35
 of neck, 43–44
Thalamus, 107
Thoracic spine, 38, 50
Tramadol (Ultram), 127
Transcendental meditation, 158
Transcutaneous electrical nerve
 stimulation (TENS), 112, 113,
 136–38
Trapezius muscle, 43, 44, 135
Trauma, 56–57, 76
Treatment, nonsurgical. *See also*
 Complementary therapies
 back's capacity to heal itself, 176–77
 bed rest, 180–81
 cold and heat, 178–80
 low-impact aerobic exercise, 201–2, 226
 rehabilitative exercise, 186–90
 resting your lower back, 182
 resting your neck, 181
 sleep, 183
 strengthening and stretching muscles,
 190–201
 wait-and-watch approach, 175–76
 waiting out acute back pain, 177–82
Treatment, surgical
 compression (osteoporotic) fractures
 and, 214–17
 criteria for, 206
 disk disease and, 208–14
 dislocations and vertebral fractures and,
 222
 elective, 203–4
 infections and, 220–21
 laminectomy, 205, 209
 lumbar spinal stenosis and, 217–18
 readiness for, 222–23
 risks and benefits of, 206–8
 spinal fusion, 218–20
 tumors and, 221
 usefulness of, 204
Trigger point injections, 135–36, 244
Trigger points, 62, 114, 135
Trunk extension, 198

Tumors
 description of, 76
 frequency and risk of, 56–57
 surgery for, 221
Tylenol, 118, 120, 122, 125. *See also*
 Acetaminophen
Type of back problem, 11–14

Ultram (tramadol), 127

Vacuuming, 237
Valium (diazepam), 128
Vertebrae
 description of, 32–33
 facet joints and, 34
 of five spinal regions, 37–38
 lumbar, 45–46
 neck, 40–42
 processes on, 33–34
 sacrum and coccyx, 50
Vertebral foramen, 41
Vertebral fractures
 description of, 56–57
 osteoporosis and, 73–74
 surgery for, 214–17, 222
Vertebrata, members of, 33
Vertebroplasty, 214, 215, 216
Vicodin (hydrocodone with
 acetaminophen), 123
Vioxx (rofecoxib), 120, 121

Walking, 201, 226
Water therapy
 acute back pain and, 201–2
 swimming, 226
Weight, healthy target, 229–31
Weinstein, James, 176
Whiplash
 defined, 60
 gentle exercise after, 184
 nerve blocks for, 132
 posture while driving and, 236–37
Willow bark, 170–71
Work hardening, 244
Work space
 setting up, 235
 sitting at computer, 22, 233–35
Workers' compensation, 241

X-rays, 87, 89–90

Yoga, 161–62

Zostrix, 130

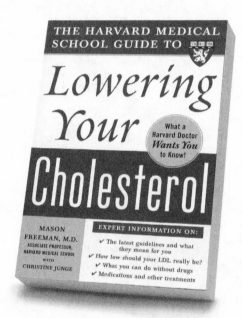
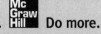